Cycling the
Kettle Valley
Railway

D1601072

Rocky
Mountain Books

Cycling the
Kettle Valley
Railway

Dan & Sandra Langford

*Front cover: Cycling through Myra Canyon's historic trestles and tunnels
(km 139, Carmi Subdivision)
Back cover: Looking out of the first tunnel in Myra Canyon
(km 137.9, Carmi Subdivision)
Title page: Trout Creek Bridge km 11.7, Princeton Subdivision (Penticton Museum)*

Maps © Dan Langford, 1994, 1997.
Photos by Sandra and Dan Langford unless otherwise noted.
Timetables and newspaper clippings courtesy of the Penticton Museum.

Copyright © Dan and Sandra Langford, 1994, 1997
2nd edition, 1997. 2nd printing 1998

The publisher gratefully acknowledges the assistance provided by the Alberta
Foundation for the Arts and by the federal Department of Canadian Heritage.

The Alberta
Foundation
for the Arts

Alberta
COMMUNITY DEVELOPMENT

COMMITTED TO THE DEVELOPMENT OF CULTURE AND THE ARTS

Published by
Rocky Mountain Books
#4 Spruce Centre SW
RMB **Calgary, Alberta T3C 3B3**

Canadian Cataloguing in Publication Data

Langford, Dan, 1959-
  Cycling the Kettle Valley Railway

ISBN 0-921102-54-2

1. Bicycle touring--British Columbia--Okanagan-
Similkameen--Guidebooks. 2. Bicycle trails--British
Columbia--Okanagan-Similkameen--Guidebooks. 3.
Okanagan-Similkameen (B.C.)--Guidebooks. 4. Kettle Valley
Railway--Guidebooks. I. Langford, Sandra, 1962- II. Title.
FC3845.04A3 1997   796.6'4'097115   C97-910164-6
F1089.O5L36 1997

CONTENTS

PREFACE

In the summer of 1991 our friends were asking about our summer plans—our reply, "Cycling the Kettle Valley Railway." Their response consistently echoed, "Where is that?" Indeed, that had been our response when reading about this rail-cycle trip in a magazine.

We were excited at the possibility of exploring this backcountry corridor, and determined to tackle it and write a guidebook so others could also enjoy this both breathtaking and at times muscle-aching adventure.

By the summer of 1993 we had returned to the abandoned railway numerous times. Over the years, the face of the Kettle Valley Railway has changed dramatically for the backcountry cyclist. Most of the rails have been removed, and some access points have either been opened or closed to the cyclist. Unfortunately, another change has been the loss of many historical landmarks that make this corridor so unique.

The labour of researching for this guidebook was full of excitement, frustration and a lot of hard work. We spent weeks cycling into the backcountry with tape recorder, camera, maps and books in hand, at times doing a lot of backtracking and making very little headway. But, as with most backcountry adventures, enjoyment often comes at the expense of hard work.

By 1996 it was evident to us that with the ongoing changes and upgrades of the railway an updated edition of the book was necessary. We welcomed a call from Robbin McKinney offering us the opportunity to partake in a cycle tour group with REM Event Management. With these return visits we were able to get valuable feedback that we could then incorporate into this edition. We are also pleased to include the Columbia & Western Railway in far greater detail with this edition, and hope it inspires many to explore this spectacular section.

While cycling both the KVR and the C&W railbeds we were delighted at the number of individuals and tour groups enjoying the rail-trail and utilizing our book as a guide. We met many local cyclists as well as couples from the USA and as far away as New Zealand. We are grateful for all the letters, email and phone calls we have received over the past few years. They have been both inspiring and informative. Once again we hope you find within these pages all that inspired us to cycle these spectacular railways.

Dan and Sandra, 1997

INTRODUCTION

The Kettle Valley Railway (KVR) is an abandoned railbed situated in the Southern Interior of British Columbia, weaving its way through the Okanagan-Similkameen region. This area has much to offer including wilderness parks, warm climate, unique towns and cities, and diverse landscapes such as mountains, rivers, canyons, orchards, lakes, sandy beaches and Canada's own desert.

The development of the Kettle Valley Railway was inspired by both the discovery of incredible mineral wealth in B.C.'s southeastern (Kootenay) mountains, as well as the fear of American domination of this region. The purpose of the KVR was to divert the Kootenay riches to the province's own seaport in Vancouver, rather than cross the border by U.S. rails.

Through the determination and ability of Andrew McCulloch, the chief engineer, the dream of a "coast-to-Kootenay" line was fulfilled, and the Kettle Valley Railway was realized. His ability to engineer the KVR through such unforgiving terrain as Myra Canyon and the Coquihalla Pass, accounted for much of the railway's reputation as an engineering marvel. These challenges were handled so skillfully by McCulloch that the railway was soon dubbed "McCulloch's Wonder." Today, you will find many commemorative plaques along this corridor recognizing McCulloch's work on the KVR.

While cycling this corridor, we find ourselves surrounded by the history of this unique railway. One example is the tunnels and trestles of Myra Canyon, reminding us of the engineering complexities and sheer labour required to see this railway to completion. While the trestles and tunnels are a sure reminder to the cyclist of the origin of this trail, you soon forget while cycling along a tree-lined railbed of green grass that 80 years ago locomotives laden with silver, copper, iron, coal and lumber began thundering over newly laid tracks.

Abandoned railway corridors hold unparalleled opportunities as recreational trails, and the KVR is no exception. This corridor is one of the most dynamic routes in the area, with some truly impressive scenery and spectacular views. The easy grade in most sections makes it suitable for either casual family cycling or easy day riding. The 600 kilometres of travel routes make it challenging for the more adventuresome. Utilizing the numerous unique accommodations and camping facilities along this route allows for weekend or extended trips.

This book provides you with a practical guide to cycling the Kettle Valley Railway. You will find detailed maps, historical information, safety tips and a kilometre by kilometre trail guide to each of the KVR subdivisions. Other useful information provided to assist you in planning your trip is the listing of local accommodations, tour operators and services. The future development of the KVR corridor is also discussed. Many groups and individuals have become active in the management of the KVR trail corridor. As a result of growing public interest and government support, we are beginning to see the conversion of the abandoned Kettle Valley Railway into a multi-use corridor that beckons the backcountry cyclist ▄▙

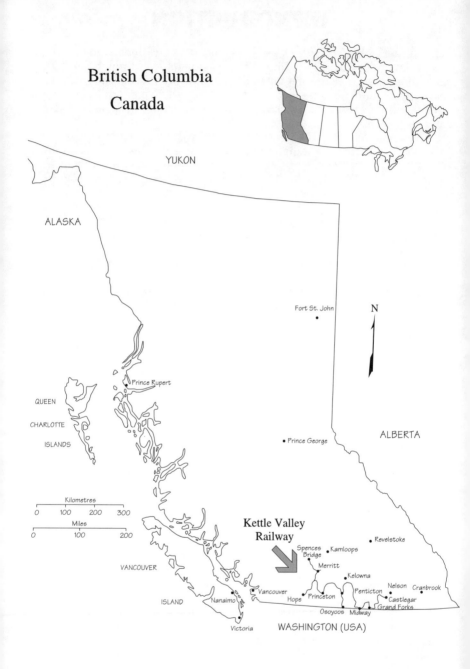

British Columbia
Canada

YUKON

ALASKA

Fort St. John

N

Prince Rupert

QUEEN

CHARLOTTE

ISLANDS

Prince George

ALBERTA

Kilometres

0   100   200   300

Miles

0   100   200

Kettle Valley
Railway

Revelstoke

Spences   Kamloops
Bridge

Merritt

Kelowna

VANCOUVER

Nelson   Cranbrook

Penticton

Vancouver   Castlegar

ISLAND   Nanaimo   Hope Princeton   Grand Forks

Osoyoos Midway

Victoria   WASHINGTON (USA)

GEOGRAPHY

British Columbia is the westernmost province of Canada covering 952,263 square kilometres of spectacular mountains, glaciers, plains, rivers, valleys, lakes, coastline and islands. British Columbia's varied landscape was created by a complex series of geological events, the first of which was the movement of land masses over the earth's surface creating mountains upon collision as well as surface volcanic eruptions at points of separation. The movement of these plates in a direction parallel to each other created the mountains and deep valleys of B.C., which have one common characteristic: each range lies with its axis parallel to the province's coastline. Rivers therefore predominantly flow in a north or south direction, each separated by one or more of the mountain ranges. A second geological event was the ice age. Evidence of the powerful erosive effects of the glaciers can be best seen in the Okanagan Valley where these glaciers crawled their way up the valleys between mountain ranges, widening the valley, grinding against rocks, and leaving glacial silt and melt water as they retreated.

These unusual geographic features have blessed this province with a wide variety of climates and scenic wonders without equal in the world. However, it has also restricted the nature of human mobility in an eastern or western direction. This has been a dominant influence in the development of British Columbia, including that of the Kettle Valley Railway. With the beginning of the KVR's construction, after years of political and corporate struggle, attention was often focused on these geographical obstacles that needed to be overcome, some of which were almost without parallel in the history of Canadian railway construction.

The route of the Kettle Valley Railway lies mainly in the Southern Interior Plateau, known as the Okanagan-Similkameen region, which is bordered on either side by mountains. To the east of the Interior Plateau is the Purcell Range of the Columbia Mountains, while to the west are the Cascade Mountains, which mark the eastern border of the area known as Southwestern British Columbia.

The Kettle Valley Railway consists of five subdivisions that make their way across 500 kilometres of mountains and valleys from the Kootenays to the coast. The Carmi Subdivision begins at an elevation of 580 metres in the town of Midway, situated in the Midway Range of the Columbia Mountains. Progressing northwest along the railbed, you climb through the Beaverdell Range of the Columbia Mountains to reach the railway's summit in the Okanagan Highlands, at an elevation of 1270 metres. The railbed then descends from the Highlands down into the Okanagan Valley of the Interior Plateau reaching Penticton at an elevation of 341 metres.

Penticton is a junction point along the KVR. The Osoyoos Subdivision progresses south from Penticton. The railbed follows the Okanagan River Valley at a relatively level grade to reach the terminus in Osoyoos at an elevation of 281 metres.

The Princeton Subdivision progresses in a northwest direction from Penticton. The KVR climbs out of the Okanagan Valley, then follows the Trout

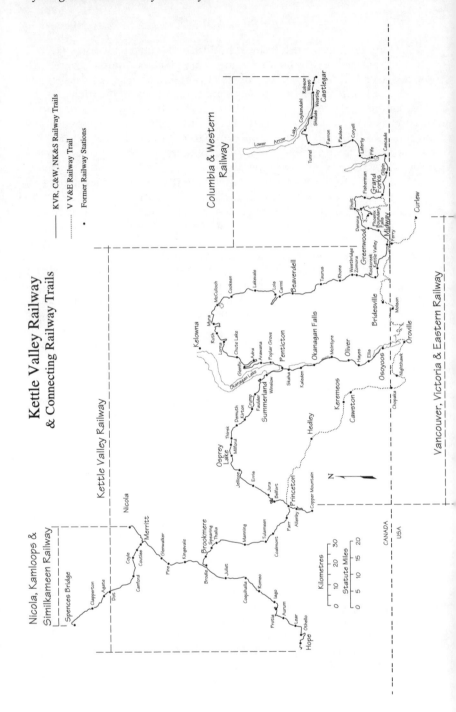

Kettle Valley Railway
& Connecting Railway Trails

— KVR, C&W, NK&S Railway Trails
····· V V&E Railway Trail
• Former Railway Stations

Columbia & Western Railway

Kettle Valley Railway

Nicola, Kamloops & Similkameen Railway

Vancouver, Victoria & Eastern Railway

Kilometres
0   10   20   30
Statute Miles
0   5   10   15   20

CANADA
USA

N

Creek Valley as it winds its way through the Cascade Mountain foothills of the Interior Plateau. After reaching the summit at Osprey Lake at an elevation of 1098 metres, the railbed descends to an elevation of 648 metres in Princeton. The Tulameen River Valley is followed out of Princeton, and the railbed climbs, reaching an elevation of 962 metres at Brookmere.

Just past Brookmere are two subdivisions, one going north and the other south. The Merritt Subdivision progresses north from Brookmere. The railbed follows the Coldwater River Valley on a gentle downhill grade to reach Merritt at an elevation of 567 metres.

The Coquihalla Subdivision progresses southwest from Brodie, following the Coquihalla River Valley through the impressive Cascade Mountains to arrive at Hope. Beginning at an elevation of 962 metres in Brookmere, the railbed climbs to 1115 metres at the summit at Coquihalla, then descends to an elevation of only 44 metres at Hope. The KVR line across the Cascade Mountains to the east of Hope was known as the most difficult and expensive piece of trackage ever built in the history of railroads.

Cycling the length of this distinctive railway enables cyclists to experience the impressive qualities that a rail-trail corridor can offer. The KVR corridor is particularly unique with its numerous trestles, bridges, tunnels, 2.2% grades, and even a couple of switchbacks and a spiral tunnel that have all been incorporated to tackle the geography of this area of British Columbia. You can certainly appreciate why geography was one reason that demanded this was to be a railway like no other ▬

CLIMATE

The climate of British Columbia can be summarized in one word—varied. One of the greatest influences on the climate is the geography. The mountains have a major effect on the weather, as the moist ocean air makes its way east across this varied landscape. For the most part, the western slopes of the Columbia Mountains and the Cascade Mountains tend to receive more precipitation, with a more arid and drier climate in the Interior Plateau. This variation becomes quite evident while cycling, for you can find snow at higher elevations, and farther down the trail bask in the sun.

The Carmi Subdivision follows along the mountains and valleys of the Kootenays, before beginning its descent into the Interior Plateau. The climate of the Kootenays is influenced by both continental and ocean air. The Kootenays have some of the same climactic characteristics as the Interior Plateau, with the exception in the higher elevations. Winters tend to be cold and dry except at higher elevations, which may have heavy rainfall in the summer and heavy winter snowfall from mid-November to April. Summers are hot, dry and low on humidity, though again, it is not uncommon for higher elevations to have an occasional July snow flurry.

Both the Princeton Subdivision and the Merritt Subdivision lie within the Southern Interior Plateau. The climate of this region is generally mild, warm and arid. Most of the summer days are dry and hot; the winters colder and somewhat wetter. However, with its proximity to the Cascade Mountains, even the occasional summer rain shower can quickly fall upon you with little advance warning.

The Osoyoos Subdivision also lies within the Southern Interior Plateau, but more importantly, it lies within the Okanagan Valley. This valley has some very distinct and unique features, such as the area between Oliver and Osoyoos that is considered Canada's only true desert and only climatic zone of its type in Canada. With an average rainfall of only 20 centimetres and temperatures ranging up to 46°C, summer days are sunny and warm, with desert nights refreshingly cool.

The climate of the Coquihalla Subdivision is influenced by the

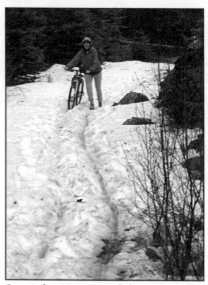

Snow in late May near Ruth, km 146.8, Carmi Subdivision.

rugged forest-covered, snow capped Cascade Mountains, and the proximity to the ocean. For about six months of every year, heavy snowfall was an extreme obstacle that often closed the Coquihalla Subdivision to rail service. It was a never ending battle for the men and their equipment to clear the tracks. Summer also presented its own problems with heavy rainfall and many washouts. It is reported that precipitation is heavier here than anywhere else in the province, with snow depths of over 12.7 metres not uncommon.

When making plans to cycle one or more subdivisions, prepare for the weather in that region. It is invaluable to the enjoyment of your trip to know the region through which you are travelling, and to be aware that weather can change rapidly in this land of mountains and valleys. For example, if cycling the Carmi Subdivision in May, you can have snow on the ground at Chute Lake, yet temperatures of 30°C in Penticton ▄▄

FLORA AND FAUNA

There is a large variety of plants and animals along the route of the KVR, such as the lush coastal growth around Hope or the more broken forests and arid land of the Interior Plateau. Because of the Pacific's moist westerly winds and the north-south mountain walls that block them, the differences in both the vegetation and animal life can be quite profound.

The Carmi Subdivision lies among the dense conifer forests of the Kootenays, with occasional open meadow areas and marshlands. The forested landscape of the Kootenays is home to a variety of wildlife—squirrels, rabbits, deer, elk, moose, bear, beaver. Sightings are common. As you descend from the summit at Myra, the heavier forested areas begin to give way to the more broken forest and semi-arid landscape of the Interior Plateau.

The Princeton and Merritt subdivisions of the Interior Plateau have more open and dry sites. The most common tree in this more semi-arid area is the ponderosa pine. Because there are more sunny openings between trees, there is room for a more varied undergrowth. Wildflowers thrive and scatter these interior forests with a wide array of colour. The rich grasslands of this region occupy the climatic zone between the desert sagebrush and the pine forested areas. Local conditions and microclimates can also create grasslands. These grasslands were never the rolling carpet of the great plains but, as in Merritt, ranching has flourished. Wildlife, including bears, moose, deer, coyotes, ground hogs and yellow-bellied marmots—to name a few, are plentiful throughout this area of the Interior Plateau.

The Osoyoos Subdivision is similar to the semi-arid drylands of the Interior Plateau, except for some distinct flora and fauna found within the desert conditions south of Oliver. This desert land is the most northern home to some typical desert wildlife such as the five-toed kangaroo rat, pocket and grasshopper mice, burrowing owls, sage cottontail rabbits, calliope hummingbirds, turkey vultures and the largest concentration of birds of prey in the country. One might also chance a rare glimpse at the turtles and rattlesnakes that wander these parts. Some typical desert plants include the sagebrush, poison ivy and the prickly pear cactus. Also commonly found in this area are plants that actually avoid living in the desert by lining the streams and sending deep roots down to the underground water table. Irrigation also changes the desert landscape to one of beautiful orchards and vineyards. However, the desert again shows its true face where artificial watering ends.

Another unique region of the Osoyoos Subdivision worth special mention is Vaseux Lake, which lies within the Vaseux-Bighorn National Wildlife Area, a sanctuary for birds and wildlife. It is home to over 200 species of birds at different times of the year. Rare trumpeter swans and other waterfowl winter on the lake, and large numbers of Canada geese nest here

yearly. On the eastern slopes above the lake you will often see the herd of California bighorn sheep that range here.

Much of the Coquihalla Subdivision enjoys a moist coastal climate. These rain forests are exceptionally damp with lush woods filled with a heavy undergrowth of ferns and mosses.

Wildlife is abundant along the KVR.

Myra Canyon. Notice new guard rails upgraded by the Myra Canyon Trestle Restoration Society.

Flowers of the shady forest tend to be shorter, more widespread, and have white blossoms as they are not attracting bees, but often depend upon ants or beetles for propagation. As light trickles through the trees and the moisture hangs in the air, you find this to be a magical place, especially while travelling the railbed from Othello toward Hope. While standing quietly, you will notice the eery quiet of these rain forests. Birds are often well above the heavy growth and most forest mammals prefer brushy woods broken by clearings. However, Hope boasts of having more than 200 species of birds and several breeds of mammals including deer, bear, coyote, cougar and mountain goat ➤

HAZARDS OF THE TRAIL

Trestles

Some trestles have been removed, and others must be detoured because of unsafe conditions. However, for the cyclist the true hazard of the trestles is self-created. There have been serious falls from the Myra Canyon trestles owing to cyclists riding instead of walking across trestles.

In September 1992, a 22 year-old cyclist, while crossing a trestle, fell from her bike to the rocks 25 metres below. Again in June 1993, a 20 year-old cyclist riding her mountain bike fell from a trestle to the rocks six metres below. She was semiconscious when a helicopter arrived at the scene to transport her to hospital. Witnesses stated the cyclist was riding slowly; however, once losing her balance, she had no time to react. Accidents like these can be avoided by walking instead of riding your bike across a trestle.

The Myra Canyon Trestle Restoration Society has installed permanent decking and hand rails on the trestles through Myra Canyon. This area of the KVR has been a main focus owing to the large volume of people exploring the canyon and the serious accidents mentioned above. Most other trestle crossings of the KVR are not planked, so if you don't want to do a swan dive from the top, be smart; stop and walk your bike.

Tunnels

Except for the Coquihalla Subdivision, only one tunnel—the spiral tunnel at Adra in the Carmi Subdivision—is presently barricaded due to unsafe conditions. Most of the KVR tunnels have some loose rockfall within them. In order to avoid accidents, we suggest you walk your bike through the tunnels because of both the decreased visibility and the unknown cycling surface. Total darkness can actually be experienced in some tunnels. The KVR steam engines have left the tunnel walls black from soot and with little reflective quality. Even a flashlight at times gives little reprieve from the blackness. Be careful where you step. With fallen rocks in places, you could easily trip or twist your ankle. If you have a lantern, that is ideal. It is also a good idea to keep your helmet on in case of rockfall from above. Livestock can also be another hazard in tunnels. Cows go into tunnels to get out of the heat of the sun. As you're walking, it can be quite unnerving to hear or see something lurking in the darkness.

Reliability of the Trail

The reliability of the KVR corridor may change from season to season and year to year. Sections of the trail can be hard to cycle after a heavy rain or a late spring thaw. New rock slides or washouts may have occurred, or there could be changes from erosion or construction. Be aware that this is a backcountry corridor with backcountry problems. However, with the planned future development of most sections, you may also find some pleasant changes en route.

Multi-use of the Trail

Throughout the KVR corridor you will meet other people using the trail. Although some areas are inaccessible to motorized traffic, other areas are not. In fact, some portions of the trail are kept weed-free and are pleasant to cycle because of the occasional vehicle traffic. Horses and hikers are also found using these trails, especially above Kelowna and Penticton. Some trail sections get fairly well chewed up due to frequent use by large horse parties, especially if conditions have been wet. Be cautious and courteous when passing horses as they can be easily spooked.

Horses are often met when cycling the railbed.

A more hazardous encounter is that of logging trucks. Many sections of the KVR are used by the forestry industry, which has created major washboarding along some stretches. If you meet up with a logging truck, stay well off the trail and away from corners. A heavily laden truck has little manoeuvrability and no way of suddenly stopping. When a truck passes, watch for sweepers (extra long logs that overhang the back of the truck by as much as six metres). On a steep road with sharp curves, these logs can sweep you right over the edge.

Being Prepared for Your Journey

Two cyclists can be on the same trip; to one it is exhilarating, and to the other it is a horrible disaster. The difference most often lies in how prepared the cyclist was for the expected and unexpected parts of the trip. Proper equipment is the first consideration. Bring what you need, what you may need and also what you hope not to need. This last group includes things like a first aid kit or even your bike helmet. Although you don't plan to fall from your bike, even a slight blow to the head from a rock or tree stump could result in a serious head injury. Proper gear helps to ensure your trip is not disastrous.

Being prepared includes not only planning, but also being physically and mentally prepared for your venture. This will enable you to deal more effectively with whatever you might encounter. As a result, things such as delays or weather changes are not likely to ruin your trip. It is also important to know how to repair your bike in case of breakdown. The repair equipment won't work by itself!

Judging the distance you can cycle is another factor in preparing for your trip. The average fully packed cyclist manages about 10 kilometres an hour, a little faster on downhill runs, and a little slower on some of the steeper detour roads. You must also take into account your down time, such as food and rest breaks, and also time spent exploring. A good day's cycle will usually average about 70 kilometres. Be sure to plan your trip keeping in mind the ability levels of your entire group.

Private Property

At the time of writing this updated edition, almost all of the right-of-ways previously owned by CPR have now passed into public hands. The only abandoned railbed profiled in this book still held by the Canadian Pacific Railway is the section of the Columbia & Western Railway from Castlegar to Grand Forks. It is the hope of all involved with rail-trails that there will be expedient development of these corridors into official multi-use trails. Until then, when cycling the sections that are private property, one should obtain prior permission. The public corridors owned by the B.C. government can be freely travelled without fear of trespassing.

Sections of the right-of-ways that have been sold or leased to private interests do exist. The majority of these occur on spurs or older abandoned lines. Pieces have also been sold or leased within the boundaries of Penticton. Since this is an ever-changing feature of these right-of-ways, it is sometimes difficult to determine ownership. Complicating the matter are adjacent landowners erecting fences and placing no trespassing signs on sections of the railbed with no real legal claim to the right-of-way. It becomes a case of trespassing at your own risk.

One other factor to consider is that the KVR bisects a number of Indian reservations. The Indian reservations around Penticton and Merritt have all regained ownership of the right-of-way through their land, and should be respected as such. Although cycling along some of these sections does still occur, one should contact the appropriate band and also be aware that cycling through private property is a venture at your own risk.

No matter who owns the land, please respect the property you cross and close all gates. Even though the adjacent landowners may have taken the unilateral action of running a fence across the right-of-way, it is best to let the issues that led to this action be worked out by the proper authorities. The main reason for the action taken by landowners is owing to the fear that unrestricted travel through their land invites vandalism, noise, fires and garbage. We who wish to preserve this corridor for public use must help relieve these fears, and not add to them ➤

Ownership of the abandoned railway corridors (Spring, 1997)

Carmi Subdivision	B.C. government
Osoyoos Subdivision	
km 0.0 - km 7.1	Penticton Indian Band
km 7.1 - Okanagan Falls	CPR
Okanagan Falls to Osoyoos	B.C. government & local municipalities, with pieces sold or leased to private interests
Princeton Subdivision	B.C. government
Merritt Subdivision	B.C. government & Indian Reserve
Coquihalla Subdivision	B.C. government
Copper Mountain Subdivision	B.C. government with pieces sold to private interests
VV&E Railway	Unknown
NK&S Railway	B.C. government & Indian Reserve
Columbia & Western Railway	CPR
Midway to Grand Forks	B.C. government
Grand Forks to Castlegar	CPR

DRINKING WATER

It is recommended not to drink from any water source without some method of purification. Often it is inconceivable that a clear, cold, rushing mountain stream is too polluted to drink. The problem is most often the presence of the organism Giardia. Millions of North Americans are suspected of having giardiasis, however, many of these may only be carriers. Carriers remain perfectly healthy showing no signs of the disease, yet can excrete Giardia cysts through their feces for months or even years. Other animals that can carry or contract Giardia include cattle, horses, dogs, rabbits, coyotes, deer and beaver (the common name of giardiasis is Beaver Fever). Symptoms that appear after seven to 14 days of incubation are weight loss, diarrhea, cramps, bloating, nasty burps, anorexia and vomiting.

To prevent your own case of the "bad-water blues," some form of water treatment is required. One method is to boil water for a minimum of 10 minutes to kill all bacteria, viruses and parasites. A second method is to use iodine tablets. Be sure to carefully follow the directions on the bottle for maximum effectiveness. One drawback to this method is a noticeable iodine taste to the water, which can be camouflaged by adding flavoured juice crystals. The third method of water treatment is to use a water filtration system. This system is strongly recommended for frequent or extended backcountry trips. With any water treatment method it is recommended to still use the cleanest water available to minimize possible contamination.

HYPOTHERMIA

Hypothermia is a condition that results from the body's core temperature dropping to a point where your body can no longer generate heat on its own. This danger is not restricted to only high altitudes or winter conditions. With a combination of rain and wind, a person who is exhausted and unprepared can quickly fall victim. Your best defence against hypothermia is to be familiar with the symptoms, prevention and management, and to take them seriously. Deaths from hypothermia are not uncommon.

Symptoms start with a feeling of coldness, but as the body core temperature drops, uncontrolled shivering begins in an attempt to warm the body. Symptoms then progress to poor muscle coordination, weakness, lethargy, impaired judgement, and finally to unconsciousness and death unless action is taken.

The prevention of hypothermia begins with being prepared and knowledgable about the contributing factors. Foremost is wet clothing from either rain or perspiration. To stay dry from rain, we simply utilize proper raingear. Unfortunately, though most people have the proper gear, they don't stop to put it on. To help prevent perspiration wetness while cycling, take layers of clothes off as needed; then to help prevent subsequent chilling, throw back on an extra layer once stopped. A combination of clothing that works very effectively together while cycling is that of polypropylene undergarments (absorbs perspiration away from your skin) and breathable Gortex outerwear (allows perspiration through the fabric while keeping wind and rain out). Be sure you also have some method of keeping equipment and extra clothes dry, such as enclosing them in a plastic bag. There can be nothing more discouraging and potentially dangerous than to stop at your camp to find your sleeping bag wet. You should always ensure you have warm, dry clothes available upon reaching your final destination.

Exhaustion is a second contributing factor that will hasten a victim's advancement toward hypothermia, as your body requires extra energy to help keep itself warm. To prevent exhaustion, avoid getting overfatigued by stopping and resting for short periods, though not long enough to get chilled. You should also take this rest time to eat small amounts of high calorie foods to help meet your body's extra requirements.

Managing hypothermia begins firstly with reducing further heat loss. Get out of the wind or wear a windproof shell, protect your head and back of neck from heat loss, and get dry clothes on. Secondly, begin core rewarming. Because the body is not adequately producing enough heat on its own, things like hot drinks (with sugar) or attempting light exercise such as walking, can generate heat within the body to raise the core temperature. Methods used to provide heat to only the outer skin, such as skin to skin warming, or sitting by a hot fire, can be helpful in the beginning stages but since it does not directly warm the inner core, it can be dangerous to someone profoundly hypothermic. This peripheral or outer skin warming causes vasodilation, and with a severely hypothermic victim, it can cause further cardiovascular collapse. Peripheral warming should therefore be delayed until the core temperature can be raised.

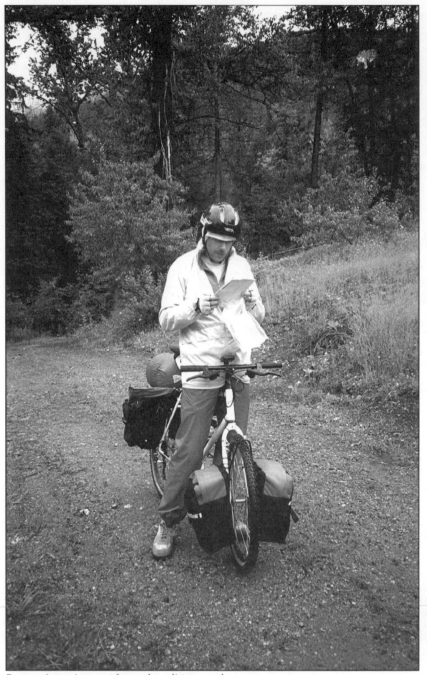

Proper raingear is a must for any long distance cycle.

Remember that the combination of wind, wetness and a state of exhaustion are all precipitating factors to hypothermia. By taking the time to prevent these and quickly responding to initial hypothermic symptoms, you can prevent yourself or your travel companion from falling victim. As a final note, in an advanced state of hypothermia, all necessary steps must be made to get medical help as this is a medical emergency ▬

HYPERTHERMIA

Hyperthermia, or heat stroke, is a condition that results when the body's core temperature is abnormally elevated and the body can no longer adequately cool itself. The advancement toward hyperthermia begins with a state of heat exhaustion, a condition we have probably all experienced to varying degrees. The symptoms of heat exhaustion are: headache, dizziness, faintness, loss of appetite, nausea, and a cool and clammy skin. The management for heat exhaustion is to remove yourself from the heat to a cooler environment and drink plenty of fluids. If unable to get out of the heat, some relief comes from wearing a head covering (the styrofoam filling of a cycling helmet works great), drinking plenty of fluids to replenish perspiration loss, wearing loose fitting clothes to allow air flow, and getting your clothes and hair wet to generate heat loss through evaporation. These actions can also help to prevent the more serious and sometimes fatal condition of hyperthermia.

If you are unable to adequately cool yourself at the stage of heat exhaustion, you may rapidly progress to hyperthermia. The symptoms of hyperthermia are an extremely elevated core temperature, warm/dry skin, visual disturbances, rapid respiration, bounding pulse, depressed level of consciousness, and possibly advancing to unconsciousness, hypotension, shock or death unless action is taken. Management necessitates you cool the person by sponging or immersing in cool water (being careful not to cool too rapidly as it may induce shivering), giving cool fluids and getting medical help as soon as possible.

Other problems that are precipitated by prolonged exposure to the sun and heat are heat cramps and sunburns. Heat cramps are muscle spasms of the arms, legs and occasionally the abdomen, resulting from an excessive loss of sodium. During times of high temperatures and heavy perspiration, sodium loss can be prevented and managed by increasing your intake of both water and sodium.

Sunburn can be easily prevented by covering your skin with clothing or sunscreen (SPF 15 or greater). The best lotions contain PABA, are nongreasy, and do not wash off easily with sweating or even swimming. Be sure to cover all exposed skin including the often forgotten back of the neck and ears. The management of sunburn begins with avoiding further sun exposure and applying cool wet compresses to the burned area. Bland creams or lotions may be helpful in first degree burns, but second degree burns, characterized by blister formations, are best managed by prolonged application of cool wet compresses or immersion in cool water and seeking medical attention if the area burned is extensive ▬

WILDLIFE HAZARDS

Bears

Both black bears and grizzly bears presently range throughout most of the Southern Interior of British Columbia. In the majority of encounters, bears avoid confrontation. In fact, if given enough warning of your approach, they will quickly vacate the area, and you may never even realize a bear was near. The long straight stretches and slow easy curves of the KVR right-of-way increases the distance at which you can see down the trail and the distance at which a bear will be aware of your approach. However, moving quickly and quietly while cycling may increase the possibility of a chance encounter. Your best protection from injury is to first try to prevent an encounter, and second, to be knowledgable about bears and the appropriate actions you should take if encountering one.

Prevention of a chance encounter begins with warning the bear of your approach. Unlike people, scent and sound are a bear's primary early warning senses. Making your presence known with the use of bells or talking will help give advance notice to any wildlife that may be on your path. However, you need to make louder noise in dense forest, as sound will not carry as far. Flowing water or wind in the forest can also muffle any noise within a short distance. Yodelling, singing or the occasional whistle blast are effective sounds that will carry a greater distance than bells or talking. The bear must be able to hear the noise while still far enough away to not feel threatened by your presence, and have enough time to leave. Although making noise is contrary to the peace we may be seeking, it may give peace of mind to know a sudden encounter with an irritated bear can be avoided.

The most dangerous bear is a garbage addicted one. Most injuries are related to garbage scavenging bears that have become conditioned to people, a more frequent occurrence as civilization encroaches farther into the backcountry. Improperly stored food and unclean campsites are contributing factors to bear encounters. When backcountry camping, always store food, garbage, and perfumed items far away from your tent and in a location inaccessible to a bear. To properly store these items, place them in air tight containers or bags to prevent excessive odours. Then store your food bag by tying it high between two trees at least 90 metres from your tent.

Prevention of injury comes from knowing the appropriate action to take when encountering a bear, and sometimes simply a little luck. A bear's actions can be somewhat understood and predicted by the existing circumstances, unfortunately all of which you may not be aware. For example, black bears and grizzly bears often react differently, as will a mother with cubs. Identifying the type of bear can at times be difficult. The colouring of both bears can range from black to blond, and the distinctive lighter coloured snout of the black bear may not be quite so evident. The grizzly bear has a distinctive hump between the shoulders, but the black bear may also appear to have a hump if its head is lower than the rest of its body. The grizzly bear is known as the more aggressive of the bears, and a mother grizzly with cubs, just as any other mammal, can be the most dangerous. If you do not know the type of bear you have encountered, assume it is the more aggressive grizzly bear.

As the KVR corridor travels through bear country, here are some steps in managing encounters with a bear:

- If the bear shows little response to your presence, try to slowly vacate the area without sudden or fast moves.
- If the bear looks directly at you panting heavily or snorting, stand your ground, again making no sudden moves. Trying to run will entice a chase, and at a speed of 13 metres/second, a bear could easily outrun you. Climbing a tree is one option, but remember black bears can climb trees better than most humans. Grizzly bears can climb, much in the same way as a human, to a height of 10 metres or reach three metres to pull you out of the tree.
- If the bear begins to charge, stand your ground. Avoid direct eye contact, but keep a close watch on the bear's movements. Although this is not easily done, most charges are false charges. The bear is attempting to determine whether you are a threat, and to let you know you are unwelcome. After false charging, usually more than once, the bear will probably vacate the area once satisfied.
- If the charge leads to an attack or you feel an attack is imminent, the accepted procedure is to play dead. Position yourself to protect your neck, face and abdomen by clasping the back of your neck with your hands, tucking your head in, laying face to the ground with your knees pulled up and keeping still. The bear may bat at you a few times to ensure you are dead and no longer a threat. Once satisfied, the bear will usually leave the area. Do not move until you are sure the bear is gone. If you fight, run or further aggravate the bear, the attack will usually continue and may lead to a severe or fatal mauling.
- The most serious of encounters is that of predation. Although it is extremely rare for a bear to prey on humans, incidents do occur. If you are being dragged through the bush after being attacked in your tent while sleeping or stalked while on the trail, you can be most certain you have been attacked as an act of predation. In this case your only chance of survival is at some point to escape.

Black bears are generally considered the more tolerant member of the bear family. If you are certain that the bear you have encountered is a black bear, further steps may be followed. Since a black bear can be easily intimidated, it can be particularly effective to show mild aggression such as throwing rocks or making loud noises by yelling or banging pots. This will usually cause the less aggressive black bear to leave or stop an attack. However, this is not recommended for a mother and cubs as it will often aggravate the bear and provoke an attack, as is true for the grizzly bear.

Remember, bear encounters are rare, but your best safety factor is your knowledge of what to do. Be sure to take steps to prevent an encounter, and be both prepared and knowledgable about bears and what action to take when encountering a bear. An excellent reference on this subject is "Bear Attacks—Their Causes and Avoidance," by Stephen Herrero.

Moose

Moose are found in many areas along the railway, especially in paralleling marshlands. Moose can be particularly dangerous during rutting season in mid-September, when provoked to aggression, or when alarming a mother with her calf. A cow moose will often initially escort the young one to a safe distance, then may return charging just as any other aggravated moose. While the majority of charges are false charges, it would be prudent to quickly clear the area and give the moose adequate room.

Snakes

During the building of the railway, rattlesnakes were one of the many hazards KVR construction workers faced. Rock blasting jolted many rattlesnakes from their rock hiding places, and many workers suffered the bite of an irritated rattler. Rattlesnakes are still found in rocks above Naramata, in fact, rattlers are abundant from Naramata to Osoyoos.

Like most wild animals, rattlesnakes tend to leave the area if they perceive you are coming. Although they have no sense of hearing and have poor sight, they are very sensitive to the smallest of vibrations and therefore will respond to approaching feet or tires. Encountering a snake while cycling on the railbed is rare, but does happen. A snake crossing your path and sensing the bike's vibration, will usually attempt to take cover with the rattler emitting a shrill high pitched hiss as it rushes away.

Because rattlers are cold blooded, they prefer temperatures between 26°C and 32°C, and will not be found hunting when ground temperatures are below 18°C. Rattlers are usually most active just before sunrise and just after sunset, when their prey of small mammals is also more active. During the heat of the day, snakes often take refuge under rocks and beneath overhanging foliage, so it is wise to avoid turning over large rocks and to be cautious when stepping into thick vegetation.

If bitten by a rattlesnake, try to stay calm. Remember that the snake has bitten you out of fright, and having been surprised and striking out in defense, may have injected little or no venom. Rattlesnakes also have a relatively low toxicity venom compared to other snakes, so if the bite cannot be treated it may only result in symptoms of dizziness, vomiting and a fever lasting up to 48 hours. First aid treatments such as cut-suck therapy are considered useless if not dangerous. Snake bite kits that involve a suction device to apply to the bite are available, but their effectiveness is questionable and should under no circumstances be used as an alternative to seeking medical attention.

Following a snake bite, the need for prompt action necessitates that the victim remains calm, relaxed and avoids any strenuous activity. An increased metabolic rate may cause the venom to spread and be absorbed dangerously fast. Foremost, seek medical attention as soon as possible.

Deer

At first you may not believe that deer could be considered a hazard, but after cycling the Kettle Valley Railway you may reconsider. Flushing deer out of the side bush is a continual nuisance that will jolt any cyclist while enjoying a peaceful ride. This quiet mode of travel allows the cyclist to sneak up on the deer. Once aware of your presence, it may bolt across the path in front of you. Sometimes the surprise or nearness of collision is enough to cause a fall. Deer are usually found in small herds. By surprising one, you may find others crossing your path a short distance down the trail. Making noise such as ringing a bell or talking, may better warn a deer of your presence, allowing it to vacate the area ahead of your arrival.

Hunters

Autumn is a beautiful and peaceful time of the year to cycle the KVR. However, it is also hunting season, which can create a hazard for cyclists in the wilderness. Hunters can be found anywhere along the length of this trail as they often use the KVR as an access route to the backcountry and to the great amount of game that are found roaming the countryside. Although the majority of hunters are responsible and cautious, accidents can and do occur with sometimes fatal consequences. If cycling during hunting season, it is necessary to wear bright colours and to make your presence known. Also, be on the watch for carrion (animal remains) from a hunter's kill, as it can attract bears and other wildlife that may attack without provocation in protection of their food source.

Mosquitoes, Ticks and Bees

The severity of insect problems varies from person to person, place to place, or even year to year. Mosquitoes, the most common nuisance, are most effectively dealt with by repellents containing DEET. Citronella repellents are also effective but for very short periods only, the advantage being they are nicer to smell, non-greasy, and can be sprayed on clothing without concern. Mosquito coils also work well if used in your tent or under a tarp.

Ticks can be a nuisance in areas where herds of large animals live. They are found on the tips of tall grasses and other vegetation and will grasp on to your skin or clothing as you brush by. Ticks will then crawl to a spot usually on your buttocks or back, and burrow into your skin to suck blood. Check yourself at least once a day for ticks if you are travelling through tall brush or grass.

Tick season is spring and summer (up to six weeks after snow has melted). Ticks commonly carry the disease Rocky Mountain Spotted Fever (RMSF). If bit, the symptoms that develop in three to 10 days are: severe head and muscle ache, fever and a measles-like rash that often starts on the feet or hands, then spreads. A tick must remain attached to the skin for about two to six hours before transmitting RMSF, so remove the tick as soon as possible. It is very important to remove the entire body because an embedded tick, even part of one, can still transmit the disease. The tick can be removed by grasping the body with tweezers and gently rolling upward. DEET type bug repellent is reputed to be effective against ticks, but if you are bitten and unable to remove the entire tick yourself, be sure to quickly get medical attention.

Bees and wasps also emerge in summer months, and anyone with an allergy to insect stings should carry medication with them at all times. Bee sting kits are available and are recommended if you are potentially susceptible ▄▄

EQUIPMENT

As with any short or long distance backcountry venture, it can be one of immense pleasure or one of exhausting agony, depending on the amount of care taken in planning. An important part of the planning is the equipment checklist. This checklist will vary, depending on when you are going, where you are going and for how long you are going. You may already have a list of what equipment you find beneficial. The following is a suggested checklist for this particular cycling trip.

Bicycle Repair Equipment
- tire repair kit (ensure glue has not dried out)
- tire levers
- Allen keys (those that fit your bike)
- wrenches (those that fit your bike)
- head set wrench
- spoke wrench
- screwdrivers
- chain breaker
- chainlinks
- oil
- *tube
- *spokes
- *freewheel removal tool
  (to replace damaged spokes)
- *crank puller
- *crescent wrench
- *cone wrenches
- *grease
- *needle nosed pliers

(*Items may be required for long unsupported trips.)

Equipment for Day Trips
- mountain bike in good working order with large tires
- cyclometer (cycle computer, so you know where you are)
- compass
- bell/whistle
- fanny pack/rear pannier
- CSA approved cycling helmet
- bicycle repair kit
- tire pump
- map(s)
- first–aid/survival kit
- stiff-soled shoes (suitable for hiking)

- cycling gloves
- windshell
- raingear
- second set of day clothes
- other clothing depending on weather, e.g., warm jacket
- sunscreen/sunglasses/sweatband/swimsuit
- mosquito repellent
- matches
- knife
- flashlight/lantern (for the tunnels)
- toilet paper and hand shovel
- water bottles (water included)
- food (some extra in case of delays)
- camera
- and foremost ... this book!

Extra Equipment for Overnight Trips
- extra clothing (polypropylene underclothing, pile jacket/pants, head covering, wools socks, extra day clothes and night wear)
- tarp (to provide shelter in sudden downpours)
- additional food (don't forget high calorie snack food)
- water purification system
- additional panniers (rear)
- sleeping bag (may also be needed at some lodgings)
- personal items (towel, toothbrush, biodegradable soap, etc.)
- waterproof bags to keep equipment dry (garbage bags work great)

Extra Equipment for Tenting
- extra tarp (to keep rain off bikes and equipment in camp)
- tent (poles, pegs, ground sheet and fly)
- rope (for hanging food between trees)
- foam pad or air mattress
- air mattress patch kit
- stove, windscreen
- extra fuel
- cooking utensils
- can opener
- dish scrubber
- towel and biodegradable soap
- panniers (front and rear)
- candles
- spare flashlight batteries
- additional food

A passenger train crosses the impressive frame trestle over West Fork Canyon Creek. This hand-crafted wooden trestle was later replaced in the 1930s with a steel bridge. (Penticton Museum)

HISTORY OF THE KETTLE VALLEY RAILWAY

In 1885 the Canadian Pacific Railway completed a Trans Canada rail line from the Atlantic to the Pacific oceans. The line across British Columbia ran far to the north, through Kicking Horse Pass, Revelstoke and Kamloops. As a result, the Southern Interior of British Columbia was almost completely isolated, with the only modes of transportation being somewhat slow and roundabout, either by steamer on Okanagan Lake or by stage to Keremeos, each then connecting to rail.

With the discovery of silver near Nelson in 1887, the potential wealth in the Kootenays was realized. The natural geography of this area enabled easy U.S. access along the north-south valleys, but it was more difficult for these riches to be transported across the province to the western Canadian centre in Vancouver.

Over the next few years, both Canadian and American railway companies surveyed possible railway routes into the Kootenays. In 1900, CPR tracks arrived from the east to the town of Midway. Between Midway and Hope lay nearly 500 kilometres of rugged mountains, so CPR's commitment to develop any farther west along this route was shaky. However, contracts for development into the Southern Interior of British Columbia were approved to an American rival, Great Northern Railway (GNR). This made the situation critical for Canadian Pacific Railway, if it was to protect its existing investment in southern B.C.

It was only through the combined efforts of J. J. Warren and Thomas Shaughnessy that the CPR was convinced to commit to the construction of a line from the Kootenays to the coast. Early in 1910, J. J. Warren became president and general manager of the Kettle Valley Railway, and shortly after, Andrew McCulloch became chief engineer. Final surveys continued under McCulloch's supervision, and construction began by 1910. This section of line would run from Midway and across the Southern Interior to Merritt, thereby connecting to the CPR main line.

The construction of this line did not come without problems. During the first year, progress moved slowly owing to a shortage of both needed materials and labour. Improvement came in 1912 when the Canadian government lifted the restrictions it had placed on workers coming into Canada from other countries. As a result, despite the sagging economic conditions of the time, the line from Midway to Merritt was half completed by 1913. Construction also commenced on the Coquihalla Subdivision.

There was a growing rivalry over the years between the KVR and the VV&E (Vancouver, Victoria and Eastern Railway, a subsidiary of the GNR), as both railways competed for access routes from the Kootenays to the coast. This rivalry resulted in battles between workers and legal battles in court. However, with the economic slump of 1913 and prospect of world war growing, increased urgency redeveloped for the completion of the entire line including that of the Coquihalla Subdivision. As a result, the VV&E and the KVR tempered their rivalry and agreed to share some trackage. The "Coquihalla Agreement" allowed the KVR to build their tracks through the

Trestle on Carmi Subdivision. In the early 1900s the Kettle Valley Railway became a lifeline linking the communities of the Southern Interior of British Columbia. (Penticton Museum)

KETTLE VALLEY RAILWAY CO.

TIME **1** TABLE

TAKING EFFECT AT 24.01 O'CLOCK

SUNDAY, MAY 30, 1915

GOVERNED BY PACIFIC TIME

FOR THE INFORMATION AND GOVERNMENT OF EMPLOYES ONLY

Miles from Brookmere	Telegraph and Telephone Offices	COQUIHALLA SUBDIVISION STATIONS	Telegraph Calls	Car Capacity Sidings
.0	DN	BROOKMERE ___ZK	BR	
4.0		BRODIE ___ZY Jct. Merritt Sub.		Nil
9.8		5.8 JULIET ___Z		35
18.0		8.2 COQUIHALLA ___ZY		70
24.1		6.1 ROMEO		39
29.6		5.5 IAGO ___Z		45
34.4		4.8 PORTIA ___ZY		46
39.8		5-4 JESSICA ___Z		46
45.2		5.4 LEAR ___Z		49
48.9		3.7 OTHELLO		70
54.3	D	5.4 HOPE ___ZY	KV	47
56.6		2.3 ODLUM ___R		Nil
		Rule 41 applies Rule 93A applies		

Courtesy of Penticton Museum.

narrow canyon of the Coquihalla, and permitted the VV&E use of these tracks by paying an annual rental fee. The "Tulameen Agreement" permitted KVR to use the VV&E tracks from Princeton to Brookmere.

In only a few years the KVR became a reality. The last spike of the Carmi Subdivision was driven on October 2, 1914. On May 31, 1915, the entire line from Midway to Merritt officially opened enabling trains to reach Vancouver by connecting to the CPR main line via Merritt. On September 28, 1915, the line opened from Brodie to the Coquihalla Station. The completion of the remaining Coquihalla line was delayed by a record snowfall of 20.4 metres in December, providing a taste of what future winters in the Coquihalla Pass would hold for the Kettle Valley Railway. However, by July 31, 1916, the Coquihalla Subdivision officially opened through to Hope, decreasing the journey to the coast.

The 61 kilometres between Hope and Coquihalla originally had 43 bridges, 12 tunnels and 15 snowsheds. Because this line was constructed during the First World War, there was a restriction of needed manpower and supplies such as explosives and building materials. Therefore, the average cost per kilometre was inflated to $84,525, five times the Canadian average during the same time period.

In the early 1920s many CPR officials suggested abandoning the Coquihalla Subdivision because of the difficulty in keeping the line open through the winter season. As a result, the KVR started a major upgrading program of the Merritt Subdivision in 1922, in anticipation of a permanent diversion to the CPR main line via Merritt. However, on January 28, 1929, a major accident occurred on the CPR main line, forcing a detour over the KVR for a three week period. The incident made the CPR management recognize the value of the KVR as a bypass route.

One of the branch lines built by the KVR was to the Copper Mountain Mine, just south of Princeton. Operations began during World War I because of the wartime demand for copper, but the mine operated for little more than a month before closing in December 1920 owing to depressed postwar copper prices. The mine and railway reopened in August 1925, providing the railway with substantial business until the Depression, forcing it to again close in 1930. Both the mine and railway would lay idle until the demand for copper increased.

A second branch line was the Osoyoos Subdivision, which transported fruit from the Okanagan Valley south of Penticton. March 1923 marked the opening of a section of the branch line from Hayes to Okanagan Falls. The fruit was then transported by barge across Skaha Lake to Penticton. In August 1931, a rail line was constructed from Penticton to Okanagan Falls, thereby eliminating the barge service.

On January 1, 1931, CPR absorbed operations of the KVR, becoming the Kettle Valley Division. Unfortunately for the CPR, this was also at the beginning of a long period of economic depression, which starved the railway of needed traffic and revenue. With the closing of Copper Mountain, an overly hot summer in the Okanagan destroying fruit crops, and numerous forest fires ravaging the Southern Interior, operation costs climbed while

Train wreck east of Iago at Coquihalla Pass. Construction problems were the norm rather than the exception. Many railway employees were killed or injured during its years of operation. (Penticton Museum)

at the same time revenue decreased. By 1933, many improvement programs were reduced along with severe cuts in operational expenses.

In September 1939, Canada entered the Second World War. Almost overnight the Depression of the 1930s gave way to a new decade dominated by the industry and commerce of war. Demand for copper, lead, coal and lumber reached new heights. With the West Coast now a significant industrial centre, Kootenay mineral traffic travelled westward. As the demand for fruit in Great Britain increased, the branch line south of Penticton was extended from Hayes to Osoyoos in December 1944, thereby completing the Osoyoos Subdivision. At one point, more than 14,000 railcars of fruit left the Okanagan annually.

In 1947, with wartime restrictions and rationing over, the CPR announced that it would undertake an ambitious program to upgrade the KVR to standards equivalent to that of the company's main line. In early 1949, oil tanks were erected at some stations, beginning the introduction of diesel-electric locomotives and the heavy movement of through freight traffic. This gave the Kettle Valley Division the earned title of "The Second Mainline."

November 1949 marked the opening of the Hope-Princeton Highway, the first of many events that changed the future for the KVR. A general drift away from using the railway for fruit shipments and for passenger service occurred, as preference for the use of the new highway grew. In 1952 the CPR announced an improved passenger schedule but to no avail. However, even with this loss, the KVR remained a busy railway during the 1950s with numerous freight trains leaving Penticton for the coast, as output of the Kootenay mines rolled westward in increasing tonnages.

HOPE LINE SLIDES
ARE CLEARED AWAY

K.V.R. Trains Which Have Been Operating Via Spences Bridge Return to Cut-off

---

Penticton Herald, November 16, 1916.

November 23, 1959, marked a second significant event, which changed the destiny of railroading in Southern British Columbia. Several washouts along the Coquihalla Subdivision resulted in temporary closure of the lines; trains were subsequently diverted via Merritt. Although this in itself was not an unusual event, the CPR decided not to repair or reopen the Coquihalla Subdivision. On January 9, 1961, CPR announced the permanent closure of the line and the last spike was removed October 24, 1962.

Along with the announced closure of the Coquihalla line was the planned rerouting of trains. The traffic from the Kootenays, which encompassed the majority of the KVR traffic, was sent north over the Lake Windermere Subdivision to Golden, and only local Okanagan traffic was sent to the coast over the KVR via Merritt. When the rerouting took effect in September 1961, more than 80% of the KVR's freight traffic vanished in a single day. On July 1, 1962, the Kettle Valley Division was abolished.

The Kettle Valley Railway was built in an age when all freight and passenger movement was by rail. The highways and airplanes of a new age stripped the KVR of its passenger, mail and high revenue traffic. The remaining bulk commodities required longer and heavier trains to remain competitive. As a result, forestry products became practically the only commodity carried on the former KVR.

By 1973, trains stopped running west of Beaverdell, and in 1978 these tracks were removed as were the tracks from the Osoyoos Subdivision in 1979. This left only the tracks from Okanagan Falls to Myra Canyon, which were preserved in an effort to maintain it as a tourist railway. Unfortunately, due to overwhelming economic difficulties, the idea was given up and the tracks removed. Announcement of the closing of the Penticton Station came in 1980, and by 1989 the last train left Merritt. In June 1990, the National Transportation Agency authorized the abandonment of the remaining line. Tracks were subsequently removed between Merritt and Penticton, except for the short section between Winslow and Faulder. These tracks remained in place for the Kettle Valley Steam Railway.

The Kettle Valley Railway will always have a special place in the hearts of those who experienced her influence. For an entire generation, it was the lifeline to the Southern Interior of British Columbia. It has been said that, due to the incredible costs of construction, operation and maintenance, the KVR never made a penny profit for the CPR. However, it has also been said that, for the people of Southern British Columbia, the untold benefit of this determined railway was the development of this region. With our past history influencing to a great extent both our present and our future, the value of this line will continue 🚂

Cycling through Myra Canyon has become increasingly popular, and why not with such incredible scenery, not to mention the historic trestles and tunnels (km 139 Carmi Subdivision)?

CYCLING THE KETTLE VALLEY RAILWAY

The Kettle Valley Railway has been an integral part of British Columbia since its beginning. With its abandonment and subsequent track removal, the opportunity now exists for the right-of-way to remain an important corridor for recreational use. The abandoned railbed of the KVR is highly suitable for backcountry cycling, perhaps becoming one of the fastest growing outdoor activities in North America.

The KVR is one of the most dynamic bike routes in the area, with nearly 600 kilometres of trail, much of which remain largely intact and open to use. Abandoned railway right-of-ways are often used by recreationists without any special improvement or upkeep. However, you may occasionally find that the reliability of the trail has changed due to such things as erosion, rock slides, fencing, construction or logging. For the true backcountry cyclist, these minor inconveniences simply add to the ultimate challenge and adventure of the trip. But if you'd rather not perform a little unplanned technical manoeuvring or detouring, you'll be pleased that many groups and individuals are committed to pursuing the restoration of this trail. Ultimately, this will ensure the availability of the corridor for years to come.

Much of the attraction of the Kettle Valley Railway is that it is a true wilderness trail, winding through B.C.'s backcountry and interconnecting various centres. The route offers some truly impressive scenery and spectacular views as you venture through a great variety of environs such as mountains, forests, lakes, desert, orchards and vineyards, not to mention the unique opportunity to guide your bike across the towering trestles and bridges, or inch your way through the darkness of tunnels.

Directly along the corridor you can also find some very unique and historic lodgings. For example, you can stay in Beaverdell at the oldest operating hotel in B.C., cook your supper by lantern light on a wood stove at McCulloch, enjoy some backcountry luxury in a rustic log cabin at Chute Lake or stay in Coalmont at an historic hotel built in 1912. Now how's that for an interesting accommodation package? But don't forget you will also find numerous scenic campsites straight off the trail.

Another great attraction to this trail is that almost all centres en route can be interconnected by bus or car, enabling you to easily return to the trailhead or make circle routes. For a pleasant four to five day circle route, park your car at Midway, cycle to Osoyoos, then bus back to Midway. Services also exist for you to fly to Penticton, then rent a mountain bike or utilize Via Rail service that travels from Jasper into B.C., stopping at locations close to the rail-trail such as Ashcroft or Hope.

Cycling the Kettle Valley Railway offers you a holiday of backcountry cycling that is quite remarkable and unparalleled. The route interconnects many unique centres of the Southern Interior of British Columbia, leading the cyclist to impressive views, beautiful scenery and fascinating places to explore. Cycling this trail is truly a dynamic and challenging venture that unfolds over the expanse of place and time ▄

Text Legend

Throughout this guide, picture keys are used as a quick reference to information about the trail, both historical and current. All measurements are in metric.

ǀ1274**Elevation**. Metres above sea level.

Station. Most stations along the KVR simply consisted of small section houses housing sectionmen and their families. Sectionmen were responsible for patrolling a section of the KVR. All that remains of these section houses are the square concrete foundations.

Water Tower. The majority of water towers on the KVR were tall octagonal structures sitting on octagonal concrete foundations. On the top was a sphere that slid up and down a pole to indicate the amount of water in the tower. The large eight-sided concrete foundations of these towers are easily found along the KVR. A few of the towers were not much more than large tanks on poles. In this case, a circle of pile footings can usually be found.

Siding. Most of the stations had sidings that are evident where the railbed becomes wider.

Spur.

Wye. For turning around engines and snowplows.

Road Crossing.

)(55x10 **Bridge**. The numbers indicate the length and the greatest height of the trestle or bridge in metres. A single number indicates the length.

Bridge Out. Any numbers following the symbol indicate the length and height of the missing trestle or bridge.

▮84 **Tunnel**. The number indicates the length of the tunnel in metres.

Camping.

Backcountry Campsite. No facilities.

Lodging.

Picnicking.

Water. Good place to stock up on water.

Backcountry Water. Water source is a stream or lake and may need to be purified.

Restaurant or Snack Bar.

Grocery store.

Bike Shop.

Hiking Trail.

Winery.

Phone.

Information Plaque.

1.0 **Uphill Grade**. The least liked symbol of the bunch. Of course, if you are going in the opposite direction this may be your favourite. A grade symbol is found at each station, the number indicates the average percent grade to the next station. Percent grade is the altitude gain (or loss) of the railway over a specified length, expressed in percent. An uphill grade of 1.0% would mean that the KVR rises 1 metre for every 100 metres of length. Grades less then 1.0% will hardly be noticeable.

2.1 **Downhill Grade**. Yes! Sit back and enjoy the scenery. Just as with the uphill symbol, the number indicates the average percent downhill grade between stations. Grades approaching 2.0% are great coasting grades.

Level Grade. The average grade between stations is less than 0.1%.

→ **Detour Off**. The KVR becomes impassable, a detour off the railway at this point is necessary. Reaccess the KVR at the Detour On symbol.

← **Detour On**. After detouring off the KVR, it is possible at this point to get back on the railway. If following the KVR from the other direction the symbols mean the reverse.

⇒ **Possible Detour Off**. The KVR is marginally passable and may require a detour.

⇐ **Possible Detour On**. If you detoured when the KVR became marginally passable, this is where you reaccess the railbed.

Map Legend (Large Scale Maps)

┼┼┼┼┼┼┼ KVR, C&W Railbed–Passable (each crosstie represents 200m)

\+ + + + + + + KVR, C&W Railbed – Not Passable

┼┼┼┼┼┼ KVR, C&W Road built on Railbed

┼┼┼┼┼┼ VV&E, Railbed–Passable

\+ + + + + + + VV&E, Railbed–Not Passable

┼┼┼┼┼┼ VV&E, Road built on Railbed

┼┼┼┼┼┼ Active Railway

———— Highway

———— Street

— — — — Gravel Road – Main

– – – – – Single Lane – 2wd

-------- Single Lane – 4wd

·············· Trail – Single Track

24.9 ——— Distance Marker (kilometres)

14.2 — Station–Distance Marker (kilometres)

⟩·········⟨ Tunnel

⎓ Trestle, Bridge

⋀ Campsite

⋀ᴮ Campsite, Backcountry

🏠 Lodging

⊓ Picnic Site

Ⲧ Winery

✗ Mine

⌒⌣ River, Creek

⌒ Contour Line – 200m interval

⌒ Index Contour Line

▬ ▬ ▬ ▬ Indian Reservation Boundary

Kettle Valley Railway
Carmi Subdivision
Midway to Penticton
215.0 km

CARMI SUBDIVISION
Midway to Penticton, 215 kilometres

The section of the KVR between Midway and Penticton is known as the Carmi Subdivision, offering 215 kilometres of delightful cycling on a well-travelled trail and a relatively level terrain. However, the distance can challenge your legs and your endurance. So, pack your panniers, pump up your tires and get ready for an exhilarating three to four day cycle trip. Oh, and if you came for the views, you won't be disappointed.

Start this trip by pedalling your fat tires along the packed gravel, beginning at the Midway Station. The railbed follows the valley of the Kettle River, passing through the towns, villages and scenic farmland of the Kootenay Boundary Country. Unfortunately, some sections have been fenced owing to ranching or farming, thus entailing a little detouring, bushwhacking and cow patty dodging. Nevertheless, this is an easy, enjoyable ride as the trail climbs gently but steadily into the Okanagan Highlands.

When you reach the near abandoned town of Carmi and the remains of the Carmi Mine, you'll want to park your bike as this historic site beckons you to explore its remains. Continuing on the packed gravel trail, you pass through this pine forested backcountry on a gentle uphill grade to reach Hydraulic Lake. Near McCulloch Station, on the shore of Hydraulic Lake, is McCulloch Lake Resort, a quaint little resort with camping and cabins that takes you back to the days of wood burning stoves and propane lights.

A near level grade lies between McCulloch and Myra, so if you want to put the pedal to the metal and work up a sweat, you can click off the kilometres, stopping short of the canyon. At Myra Canyon the views abound, and as you cross over the many trestles and through the tunnels, you are again reminded that you're cycling in the tracks of an incredible railway.

Once out of the canyon, your ease of pedalling soon makes you aware of the gentle downhill grade. With gravity as your ally, the next thing you know, you're at Chute Lake. The lodge located here is a beautiful log building set next to the lake. You'll almost believe it's a mirage after such a remote stretch of backcountry. Cyclists are more than welcome, be it for a piece of Doreen's famous homemade pie, or a few days of R&R.

Leaving Chute Lake, the downhill grade significantly increases as you descend into Penticton. The trail is generally in good shape for a multi-use trail, i.e., hikers, cyclists, motorized vehicles, horses and cows! Some logging roads intersect the railbed at various points; if tempted to follow, be ready for a wicked descent. Don't be in too much of a hurry, or you will miss the impressive views of the Okanagan Valley. Once you've reached Penticton, you'll wonder why you went so fast.

The end of the trail awaits you in the attractive city of Penticton, nestled between Okanagan and Skaha lakes. Penticton was named by the Indians, meaning: a place to stay forever, and that's just what you may want to do. All conveniences are found here, and it is a great spot for a refreshing dip on a hot day. Who could pass that up after having just cycled 215 km?

Kettle Valley Railway - Carmi Subdivision
km 0.0 - km 17.2

km   **Midway Station** ⎸580 ◼ ⬤ ⧘ ⧘ Y ⅄ ⬛ ⧓ ⬤ ⧘ ⬤ (⎺⎺0.1
0.0

Midway is a town named for the fact that it is halfway the distance across British Columbia. This was a town of much activity during the railway boom as it was a junction point for railways both going and coming from the east and west, and also south from across the border.

The original Midway Station was declared a heritage site and purchased by the Kettle River Museum. The station was then moved a few hundred metres southwest of the original site onto land owned by the Village of Midway. The large sugar maple now northeast of the station was planted from seed by Mrs. Nichols, wife of KVR agent Henry Nichols, to shade the station from the summer sun. Today, the railway station still serves the public as a museum where much of the history of the KVR can be found. The railgrade in front of the Midway Station is wide and clear.

West of Midway on the VV&E line is the site at which GN crossed over CPR land in 1905. This incident resulted in the CPR and J. J. Hill's Great Northern Railway fighting the Battle of Midway. The disputed area is five kilometres west of Midway across the Kettle River on the old grade of the VV&E.

0.9   Highway #3. ⬈

2.8   Pope and Talbot Ltd.—Midway Sawmill ⧘⇒

In 1905, the Midway and Vernon Railway (M&V) constructed a grade from the sawmill to Rock Creek in an attempt to secure government grants. The KVR, in an intimidation move, continued its line from Midway to km 4.0. With the failure of the M&V, the KVR continued westward utilizing the already constructed grade of the M&V. The original M&V grade can be seen about 30 metres to the north, paralleling the KVR grade. At km 4.0 the KVR shifts onto the original M&V grade.

The KVR grade lies next to Midway Sawmill's property and has been removed or blocked by fences. A detour will be required due to the continually changing status of the railbed through the Midway Sawmill.

41

Midway was a busy town during the railway boom. Today, the original KVR station is a museum.

Midway Museum
(Highway 3, Midway, 250-449–2413)

The Battle of Midway

It was in November 1905, in the tiny town of Midway, British Columbia, that the battle between railway rivals James J. Hill of the Great Northern Railway (GNR) and William Van Horne and Thomas Shaughnessy of the Canadian Pacific Railway (CPR) was to come to physical blows.

The rivalry between these two railways began before the construction of the CPR transcontinental line to Vancouver. Hill and Van Horne, then directors of the CPR, disagreed on the route the CPR would take to the western shores of Canada. Hill, a Canadian by birth, wanted the line south through the United States and north to Winnipeg, thus avoiding the costly construction through the rocky Canadian Shield north of Lake Superior. But Van Horne, ironically an American, wanted an all-Canadian route. The majority of CPR directors supported Van Horne's all-Canadian route, infuriating Hill. Hill left the CPR and Canada, swearing revenge against Van Horne and the CPR.

In the years that followed, Hill, with the GNR, attempted to gain control of railways into Canada. He was out-manoeuvred each time by Van Horne, who would not allow an American railway into Canada. In retaliation, Hill drove tracks from Seattle to Vancouver only to be stopped 20 miles short owing to a lack of funding for a bridge over the Fraser River.

His next assault was the successful venture with the Kaslo and Slocan Railway (K&S) in 1895, building a line over the mountains to reach the silver mines of Sandon.

At Sandon, there was a conflict regarding the ownership of land on which the Nakusp & Slocan Railway (N&S) had built their CPR station. In retaliation the K&S men tore down the CPR station and freight shed.

Skirmishes and legal battles between the two railways were common place. In 1899, Shaughnessy, another American by birth, succeeded Van Horne as president of the CPR and continued on with the fight to restrict Hill from getting a foothold into Canada. Of course, this did not stop the CPR from teaming up with Daniel Corbin to drive a rail spike deep into the heart of Hill's Spokane railway monopoly, building a railway from Spokane to the CPR main line and diverting rail traffic bound for the Eastern United States over the CPR main line. Corbin had lost his own railway, the Spokane Falls and Northern Railway to J. J. Hill years earlier. Hill did not take this lying down and put his financial backing into the floundering Vancouver, Victoria and Eastern Railway (VV&E).

The VV&E was chartered in 1896 by William Templeton, mayor of Vancouver, in order to build the coast-to-Kootenay railway to ensure that the riches of the Kootenays would find their way to Vancouver and not into the boxcars of J. J. Hill's GNR. Although there was a general distrust of Hill's promise to build the "coast-to-Kootenay" line, Hill was granted an amendment to the VV&E's charter allowing it to divert through the U.S. in order to complete the line to the coast. The CPR responded immediately by dispatching its surveyors to survey a completely Canadian route from the coast to the Kootenays.

As the grade for the VV&E pushed through west of Midway, it inadvertently crossed a small parcel of land granted to the CPR. On September 30, 1905, the CPR erected a fence across the grade, claiming the VV&E was trespassing. Hill managed to get an expropriation order for the parcel of land, which the CPR immediately claimed invalid and not for the parcel in question. On November 7, 1905, Hill massed an army of workers to the disputed property. The CPR responded at once, by ordering all available railway workers to Midway. Hill, hearing of CPR's move, dispatched additional troops to Midway. On November 9, the brigade of CPR workers armed with shovels, picks and axes massed against the formidable VV&E. Tracks were torn up, shovels and picks clanged against one another, and shots were fired. Miraculously no one was killed. Nightfall put an end to the day's hostilities. The next morning the CPR workers found the disputed area barbwired. Not wishing to contend with the barbwire without wire cutters, the CPR workers headed for the saloons in Ferry, just across the border. There the hostilities ended with the VV&E and CPR workers standing shoulder to shoulder at the bar. In court the CPR was found to be correct, and Hill had to get an expropriation order for the right parcel of land.

The KVR winds along the shoreline of the Kettle River, km 13.4.

The first trestle of the KVR crosses the Kettle River to Kettle River Provincial Park, km 24.9.

3.7   Far end of Midway Sawmill |⇐

KVR grade after this point runs through cow pastures and can be rough in places.

4.9   Gate easy to open.

5.7   Gate at end of field.

6.2   Gate, difficult to open, may require lifting bikes over. Until km 8.7 cows and cow patties are obstacles, as the railbed has been incorporated into a cow pasture.

8.7   Highway #3 |→

KVR crosses under the bridge of Highway #3. The railbed becomes impassable due to rock slides and heavy growth of weeds, while farther down the line, the grade has been ploughed under.

After crossing under the Highway #3 bridge, detour to the east on to Bubar Road. Most of the railway grade past this point to km 13.4 has been ploughed under by adjacent landowners. Small sections of the right-of-way can be seen paralleling the river from Bubar Road. Bubar Road connects with the KVR at km 13.4. The detour is 4.2 kilometres.

An alternative to using Bubar Road is to detour west on Highway #3. Turn on to Kettle Valley East Road, and at the elementary school turn north on to Kettle Valley South Road, crossing over the Kettle River on a one-lane bridge. The road then intersects the KVR just on the other side of the river at km 14.2. The railbed appears as a one-lane road.

13.4   Bubar Road connects with KVR. |⇐

14.2   Kettle Valley Station |595 🚋 ⳾ 🚲0.2 |→

The name "Kettle" River originates from the large whirlpools found along the Kettle River.

West of the intersection of Kettle Valley Road South, the right-of-way becomes an access road to a farmer's residence and fields. Past the farm, the railbed has been ploughed under. Detour north on to Kettle Valley South Road to km 16.1. The detour is 2.7 kilometres.

16.1   Jim Blaine Memorial Park Δ |⇐

Overnight camping, sports ground and playground. Past the campground the KVR railbed becomes part of the Kettle Valley South Road.

17.9   Abandoned sawmill.

18.2   Rock Creek Station |603 🚋 ⳾ 🏛 ⚲ 🍴 🚲0.2

Named after the community of Rock Creek that already existed here when the KVR came through. The community of Rock Creek was born when gold was discovered in the small creek that enters the Kettle River here. Rock Creek Park (day use only) is across the Kettle River and 300 metres south on Highway #3.

2

Kettle Valley Railway - Carmi Subdivision

km 12.3 - 38.2

N

19.0   Detour ╎➔

The road branches from the railbed to the east, and parallels the KVR. The railbed itself is overgrown and not easily passable. Detour by following the road that narrows and ends at some residential properties. Re-access the KVR on the west. The detour is 2.4 kilometres.

21.3   Detour reconnects with KVR. ╎◄

22.8   Gate ╎➔

A locked metal gate with an eight foot-high electric fence surround a local property and the adjacent railbed. A rough road skirts along the east side of the enclosure. The electric fence has no purpose other than to keep cyclists from crossing the railbed that cuts through this person's property. If approaching from the other direction you will find yourself on the other side of the gate surrounded by the high electric fence. The railbed can be reaccessed with some difficulty at the end of the electric fence at km 23.4 or the road can be taken to km 24.7.

23.4   Rough access ╎⇐

Requires throwing bikes over the old railway fence.

24.7   Road reconnects to KVR. ╎◄

24.9   Kettle River)(72 ᚛

A through truss bridge crosses the Kettle River entering Kettle River Provincial Park. On the west side of the river is a refreshing picnic site, complete with sandy beach and swimming hole. The KVR bisects the Kettle River Provincial Park, which offers overnight camping to the north of the right-of-way and picnicking to the south.

25.2   Park road to overnight campground. ⵢ ▮ Ⴞ

25.9   Rock slide

A small rock slide from a cut in the out-cropping rock covers the railbed. A passable trail winds through the rock slide.

26.1   Gate

From here to Zamora the KVR runs through farm fields and is gated at km 26.1, 27.0, 28.5 and 29.3. Please be courteous and close all gates behind you.

28.5   Ed James Creek

The creek has washed away the railbed and added a technical challenge to the route. Easily walked over.

30.4   Zamora Station ╎624 🚊 ⵢ ⵢ 🚲 ╎⇒

Named after the Spanish province of Zamora. To reach the small community of Zamora you pass through farmers' fields and a couple of gates. The original station house is still standing alongside the KVR, and is presently used as a private residence.

3

57.8
57.5
56.6
52.0
50.5
Taurus
47.6
47.0
46.5
46.0
44.4
43.2
42.8
38.2
38.0
39.9
Rhone

Big Goat Creek
Little Goat Creek
Dominion Creek
Boyer Creek
Taurus Creek
Hay Creek
Creek
Kelly
Nelse Creek
West Kettle River
River
33

Kettle Valley Railway - Carmi Subdivision
km 37.9 - 59.4

0   1   2   3   4 km
0   1   2   3 miles

N

At Zamora, continuation on the KVR becomes troublesome due to three ungated fences in the next 0.7 kilometres. Depending on the season, the right-of-way can also be overgrown with tall grass, making travel somewhat difficult. A 2.5 kilometre detour on the highway to Westbridge may be a preferred option. To detour, take Zamora Road to Highway #33 and follow it to Westbridge. The railbed can be seen from the road. It is possible to again reconnect with the KVR using Dez Mazes Road but the railbed is only marginally passable to Westbridge from there.

31.1   After a wooden fence, the right-of-way is used as an access road by local residents and is well-maintained.

32.4   Dez Mazes Road † ┊⇒ ┊⇐
After another wooden fence, the KVR is again grassy with some tree growth and passability will depend on the season. An option is to detour on Dez Mazes Road to Highway #33 and follow it to Westbridge.

33.0   Westbridge Station ┊625 🚂 🛉 ⫽† 🛉🍎(🚲0.4 ┊⇐
The remains of the station are found just before crossing Highway #33. Evidence of the water tower was erased when the highway was relocated. Westbridge General Store is located on the highway across the river. The railbed leaving Westbridge is a well-packed single lane gravel road.

33.1   Highway #33 and Westbridge Road. †

37.3   Cattle guard.

38.0   Blythe-Rhone Road † ┊→
Detour west (left) on Blythe-Rhone Road to Rhone, as the bridge that crosses Conkle Creek is out. Following the crossing of Conkle Creek, the right-of-way is weedy and bisected by numerous fences. Detour is 2.7 kilometres.

38.2   Conkle Creek ⋊14

39.9   Rhone Station ┊652 🚂 ┊ 🚲0.8 ┊←
Named after the Rhone River in France. The foundation of the Rhone Station is found 200 metres south of the intersection of the Blythe-Rhone Road and the KVR. On the west side of the road is a local World War II memorial. For the next 2.7 kilometres the Blythe-Rhone Road uses the grade of the KVR.

42.8   KVR and Blythe-Rhone Road depart ┊⇒
The bridge crossing the West Kettle River at km 43.2 has been removed. The more adventuresome may want to continue on the KVR and wade or boulder hop the West Kettle River. Otherwise continue to follow the Blythe-Rhone Road across the river. From the road bridge crossing the river, the abutments of the old railway bridge are visible 400 metres downstream. 0.9 kilometres past the bridge, the Blythe-Rhone Road again crosses the railway, before intersecting with Highway #33.

Bull Creek Canyon, km 47.2.

Beaverdell Hotel, no doubt one of the busiest hotels during the railway boom, is now the oldest operating hotel in British Columbia, km 68.1.

43.2   West Kettle River ▮ᴮ ⌗ *30*

Although the bridge is missing, the river can be forded during low water levels. The original railway bridge over the West Kettle River was removed and is being used as a bridge for the Blythe-Rhone Road seven kilometres downstream.

44.4   Blythe-Rhone Road ⌕ ⫣⇐

Take the KVR on a beautiful and scenic ride to Taurus. This section also has many spots along the river that lend themselves to backcountry camping.

46.0   Slide area that is easily passed over.

46.5   Access road to Highway #33. ⌕

47.0   Bull Creek Canyon

Here the West Kettle River cuts a deep gorge through a rocky obstruction in the valley. The original surveys for the KVR suggested that a tunnel be forged through the ridge on the west side of the river. McCulloch, not wanting to waste time and money on tunnel construction, relocated the survey to cross the West Kettle River and hug the east wall of the canyon, thereby avoiding the tunnel. This required two bridges across the West Kettle River.

47.6   West Kettle River. Δ^B ▮ᴮ)(*33*

50.5   Taurus Station ▮*714* ▰ ▮ ▯ ⚓*0.4*

Originally named Bull Creek Station, the station was renamed Taurus, after the astrological sign of the bull, to avoid confusion with another CPR station named Bull River. The site of Taurus Station is marked by the large octagonal cement foundation of the water tower and the cement foundation of the station house.

50.6   Little Goat Creek. ▮ᴮ)(

52.0   Moose crossing

This marshy area is a particularly good spot to find moose.

56.6   Rainbow trout wild hatchery. Δ^B ▮ᴮ ⌐

57.5   Short trail to the river.

57.8   **Water tower—Big Goat Creek** ▮ ▮ᴮ)(

On the south side of Big Goat Creek lies the remains of a water tower and a small shed. The only evidence left of this water tower are pieces of foundation and supporting cables coming out of the ground. A small red KVR shed is back in the bushes to the east, and a small trestle crosses over Big Goat Creek.

Logging traffic has reduced spots of the railbed to washboard.

Carmi
75.0

75.5

74.6
74.8

74.2

33

4

71.1

Beaverdell
68.1

68.8

Beaverdell

66.4

West Kettle River

64.8

Dellwye
63.4

61.5

61.2

Kettle Valley Railway - Carmi Subdivision
km 55.6 - km 75.6

0   1   2   3   4 km

0   1   2   3 miles

N

57.8
57.5

56.6

61.2   Tuzo-Eugene Forest Service Road. ⌁

61.5   Tuzo Creek ⬛)(14

Tuzo Creek was named as a memorial to the sacrifice of J. A. Tuzo, an assistant engineer on the KVR, who was among the first Canadians to be killed in World War I.

63.4   **Dellwye** Y

A wye was built here to turn around snowplows that were used between here and Penticton. The name was formed from a combination of Beaverdell and wye. Although grassy, the wye is a well-defined cut into the trees.

64.8   KVR parallels Beaverdell Station Road.

66.4   Beaverdell Station Road ⌁

From here, the Beaverdell Station Road uses the railgrade for the next 1.8 kilometres. The road passes a sawmill and an abandoned mill that once processed ore from the Highland Silver Mine. The Silver Mine is 500 metres above Beaverdell on Wallace Mountain.

68.1   Beaverdell Station |787 🚂 ⸸ Λ ⛺ ⍕ ⵏ ● ⬤ (♿0.9 |→

Evidence of both the station and right-of-way are lost in the middle of what are now large tailing ponds. The station was situated at the point where the Beaverdell Station Road turns east toward Beaverdell. Detour following Beaverdell Station Road east for 300 metres. Just past Kettle Valley Welding Limited, turn north on to a one-lane trail that leads around the east side of the tailing ponds. The trail turns on to the railbed 0.8 kilometres from Beaverdell Station Road.

If you continue down Beaverdell Station Road to Beaverdell you ride over West Kettle River on the railway bridge that was used to carry the KVR over Wilkinson Creek at km 81.2. Located at Beaverdell is the oldest operating hotel in British Columbia, the Beaverdell Hotel. A community campground is on the edge of the river, just north of the bridge across the Kettle River. This interesting community makes a great stopover point and is the last place before Penticton for stocking up on food and supplies.

68.8   North end of tailing ponds |←

The one-lane trail that leads around the tailing ponds connects to the right-of-way.

71.1   KVR crosses the open valley bottom of the West Kettle River.

74.2   Entering Carmi.

74.6   Carmi Mine ⚒

Jim Dale staked the Carmi mine in 1896 and named the area after his Illinois home town. Prospering from the gold mine and a 10 stamp mill,

When the gold mine closed in 1939, Carmi became a near ghost town. This hotel was one of two in the town, km 74.8.

Fording Wilkinson Creek, km 81.2. Photo: Robbin McKinney.

the town boasted two hotels, a jail, hospital, two stores and gas stations. With the closing of the mine in 1939, residents moved on. Today all that remains is a near ghost town.

Evidence of Carmi can be seen on both sides of the right-of-way as you approach the mine buildings. A main street ran parallel to the west side of the KVR, with piles of wood left to mark the location of most buildings.

74.8   Carmi Creek

One of the abandoned Carmi hotels is still standing and can be seen down the hill to the east.

75.0   Carmi Station |847 🚌 📦 ┃ 🚲0.9

Pine trees now grow from the middle of the station's foundation, and across the KVR from the station site is the water tower foundation. The present–day residents of Carmi live in houses to the east of the railbed.

75.5   Carmi Creek Forest Service Road ↑ ⇒

The bridge crossing Wilkinson Creek at km 81.2 is out, requiring you to ford the creek. During low flow rates in late summer this is easily accomplished. If able to cross the river, the railbed to Lois is well travelled and in very good condition.

If the river is high and fast, or you don't want to get your feet wet, detour east on Carmi Creek Forest Service Road and then turn north on Highway #33 and cross Wilkinson Creek. Once across the bridge, turn west on to Wilkinson Creek Forest Service Road. Follow this road for 500 metres and you will find on your right a 4x4 path that reconnects you to the KVR. This 4x4 path branches, with the left branch being the most direct route to the KVR and the other branch rejoining the KVR at Lois. Both paths gain 100 metres in altitude in less than a kilometre. The detour is 2.4 to 2.8 kilometres depending on the path chosen.

81.2   Wilkinson Creek—Wilkinson Creek Forest Service Road ↑ ⚠ 🏕 ╳24

The bridge over this creek is out, but may be easily forded just downstream from the missing bridge if water levels are low. This bridge is now in use at Beaverdell as a road bridge crossing the West Kettle River. Just across the creek, the KVR crosses Wilkinson Creek Forest Service Road. The KVR grade to Lois appears much steeper then it really is, as the river valley falls and the railbed climbs.

84.3   Access road to Wilkinson Creek Forest Service Road.

86.4   4x4 path ↑ ⇐

4x4 path from Wilkinson Creek Forest Service Road intersects the KVR.

87.2   Lois Station |955 🚌 ┃ ↑ 🚲0.9 ⇐

A small shed, the concrete foundation of the station house, and a rock retaining wall are what remain of Lois Station. The second 4x4 path from the Wilkinson Creek Forest Service Road intersects here.

5

Kettle Valley Railway - Carmi Subdivision
km 75.5 - km 105.2

90.5   Small access road to Highway #33. ⵜ

92.5   Rock slide

A small rock slide is easily negotiated. It was in this section that an eastbound freight ran into a rock slide that blocked the line from April 12-18, 1925.

95.4   Creek wash covering KVR.

98.5   Lakevale Station |1053 ⬛ ▮ Ⳇ Λ ▮ᵦ 🚲₀.₉

The remains of the station house and water tower's concrete foundations are found here. This station was originally named Arlington, after the lakes of the same name, but was later changed because a station of the same name was on the Esquimalt & Nanaimo (E&N) rail line.

On the shore of Arlington Lakes is Arlington Lakes Campground, a small wilderness campground across from Lakevale Station.

99.7   Arlington Lakes Road. ⵜ

101.2 Grass and trees—road ⵑ⇒

The next 160 metres runs through a rock cut that is overgrown. The single track through this section can be quite wet. Following the road to the east (right) will avoid this spot.

101.4 Other side of grass and trees. ⵑ⇐

105.2 Wolf Creek

The KVR crosses Wolf Creek on a large fill.

106.0 Small access road to Highway #33. ⵜ

108.8 Cooksen Creek

A large fill replaced the previous trestle in 1942. The fill has washed away and a small road that itself is washing away skirts around the missing fill. Remains of the original trestle can still be seen far below.

113.2 Cooksen Station |1184 ⬛ ⳇ 🚲₀.₇

Cooksen was named after a local pioneer and rancher. A small red shack remains to indicate the location of Cooksen Station.

117.7 Scenic views of West Kettle River Valley.

118.1 Okanagan Falls Forest Service Road Λ ⛺

4.2 kilometres west on Okanagan Falls Forest Service Road is Idabel Lake Resort, which offers many services such as a restaurant, camping, lodging, a store, horseback riding and many other recreational pursuits.

120.4 Summit Lake Λᴮ ▮ᵦ

Pleasant campground, used often as a staging area by horseback riders.

N

124.4

123.4

123.0

122.2

121.8

121.4

120.4

McCulloch

Hydraulic
Lake

Summit
Lake

117.7

118.1

Haynes
Lake

Idabel

Lake

Cooksen

113.2

Kettle Valley Railway - Carmi Subdivision
km 104.8 - km 128.8

| 0 | 1 | 2 | 3 | 4 km |

| 0 | 1 | 2 | 3 miles |

Devil Cr

108.8

106.0

6

121.4 Hydraulic Lake Campground Δ ⓑ

Relaxing campground within the trees and along the shore of Hydraulic Lake.

121.8 McCulloch Lake Resort and Campground Δ ⓐ ⓘ

Open year round, the resort has quaint little cabins and a camping area on the shore of Hydraulic Lake. The facility includes showers, fishing, boating, X-country skiing and canoeing. It is very rustic, like a step back in time with wood cook stoves and propane lights in the cabins.

Past McCulloch Lake Resort the KVR can become marginally passable depending on the season and the weather. Also, there are a few cross fences between here and just past McCulloch Station. This section can be bypassed using McCulloch Road and reaccessing the KVR at km 122.2.

122.2 Access road to McCulloch Road. ⵏ

Cutting the corner of Hydraulic Lake with a causeway, the KVR creates a lagoon to the north.

123.0 Access road to McCulloch Road. ⵏ

123.4 McCulloch Station   ｉ1265 ⬤ ⓘ Ⲩ ⫽ ⚲

On May 31, 1915, at a Penticton banquet in celebration of the opening of the Midway to Merritt line, it was announced that the station at Hydraulic Lake would be renamed McCulloch to honour the Kettle Valley Railway's remarkable engineer, Andrew McCulloch.

Foundations can still be seen. Past the station, the railbed is used by logging trucks. Evidence of logging is visible all along the KVR to Myra Station.

124.4 Access road to McCulloch Road. ⵏ

135.2 Myra Forest Service Road ⵏ

Used as an access road from Kelowna for day trips into Myra Canyon. This is not an easy road to cycle because of steep grades and loose rock. It is 8.5 kilometres down to McCulloch Road.

135.3 Myra Station   ｉ1270 ⬤ ⫽ ⫽ ⚲0.2

Myra was named after the daughter of engineer J. L. Newman. The cement foundations from the station are found here. Just past the station, the railway enters a canyon where it hangs on the sides of cliffs, crosses numerous trestles and travels through two tunnels. The area between Myra and Ruth is now commonly known as Myra Canyon. This canyon forced the railway to wind into the canyon on a wide detour.

Many of the original trestles were filled in during the upgrading of the railway in 1929. Two of the trestles were replaced with steel and the remaining wooden trestles refitted with new lumber. When the wooden trestles were originally constructed, each timber was cut and bored by hand. No shims were permitted, the fitting had to be exact.

Kettle Valley Railway - Carmi Subdivision
km 128.9 - km 163.5

This 132 metre-long frame trestle marks the summit of the Carmi Subdivision at an elevation of 1274 metres at km 138.22.

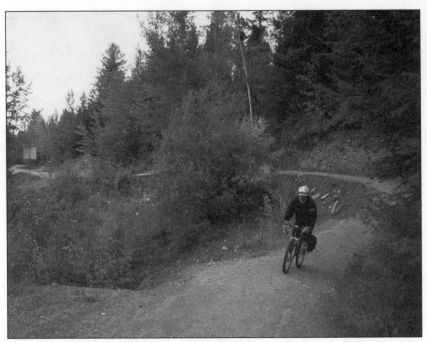

Entering Myra Canyon, the trail skirts a washout, km 135.9.

The first tunnel in Myra Canyon, km 137.96.

Myra Canyon has changed over the past few years. When we first cycled this section, all trestles were easily walked over. Subsequent trips proved to be somewhat disappointing as vandalism and age was making passage more difficult. We were therefore very pleased to find that progress was underway to restore and upgrade this most spectacular section of the Kettle Valley Railway.

The Myra Canyon Trestle Restoration Society is the group largely responsible for the upgrading and maintenance of the KVR corridor through Myra Canyon. The changes in Myra Canyon are to enable this corridor to meet the British Columbia provincial standards for park status. Some of the work involved covering the original trestles with decking and the installation of handrails. While this can detract from some of the excitement of looking down through the ties to the ground many metres below, the potential excitement has been exchanged for safety.

Myra Canyon could have never been considered a corridor safe for travel in the condition to which it had declined. In fact, a few people have fallen from the trestles resulting in very serious injuries. Now upgraded, Myra Canyon, just as the Quintette Tunnels at Othello, can be added to British Columbia's long list of provincial parks.

135.8   Parking and outhouse
The main parking area for day-exploring Myra Canyon.

135.9   Washout
The trail skirts around the washout.

136.2   Cut in rock
In the initial stages of construction, this was to be a tunnel. However, upon encountering loose rock near the centre of the tunnel, a decision was made to excavate a deep cut instead. Dynamite, which had replaced black powder, was just starting to be used when the KVR was being built. Its use presented a major problem in that the dynamite readily froze under the winter conditions. Due to carelessness and lack of experience many fatalities resulted from workers attempting to quickly heat dynamite in frying pans.

136.76   Frame trestle #18)(55x10
The Myra Canyon Trestle Society numbered the 18 trestles in Myra Canyon from west to east.

137.16   Frame trestle #17.)(27x8

137.22   Frame trestle #16.)(27x12

137.27   Frame trestle #15.)(46x12

137.48   Frame trestle #14.)(73x12

Kettle Valley Railway
Myra Canyon - Carmi Subdivision
km 134.1 - 144.9

137.73 Frame trestle #13.)(87x15

137.81 Frame trestle #12.)(24x10

137.96 Tunnel. 114

138.22 Frame trestle #11)(132x24
This is the summit of the Carmi Subdivision at 1274 metres.

138.91 Tunnel. ◼84

139.03 Frame trestle #10.)(59x9

139.28 Klo Creek—East Fork Canyon Creek Bridge #9)(111x48
This was originally a frame trestle, changed when CPR upgraded the line. The present bridge consists of five steel through-plate girder spans on steel towers.

Hand-fitted loose rock retaining walls preceed the abutments of most of the trestles in Myra Canyon, km 137.22.

139.41 Outhouse.

139.42 Frame trestle #8.)(73x21

139.68 Bench overlooking the second tunnel and trestle #10.

139.80 **Water tower** 🕯
The concrete foundation blocks are still here.

140.81 S-Curve frame trestle #7.)(90x25

141.50 Pooley Creek—West Fork Canyon Creek Bridge #6)(220x55
This is the longest and highest bridge in Myra Canyon. Originally a frame trestle, it was replaced in 1931-32 with steel. The bridge consists of twelve steel through-plate girder spans on steel towers.
This is the site where the last spike was driven for the Carmi Subdivision on October 2, 1914. On October 6, the first train ran from Penticton to Midway. Regular service started May 15, 1915 with the completion of the line to Merritt. Fifty-eight years later in June 1973, the final train operated over the tracks in Myra Canyon when the Canadian Broadcasting Corporation filmed segments of "The National Dream."

141.74 Frame trestle #5.)(23x3

141.89 Frame trestle #4.)(150x37

142.40 Frame trestle #3.)(82x9

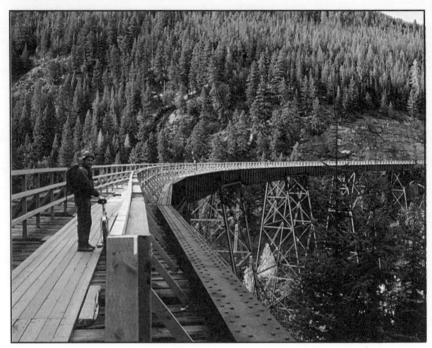

West Fork Canyon Creek Bridge, km 141.50.

Chute Lake Resort, km 171.5, is a welcome sight for weary cyclists.

142.6   The KVR was relocated, diverting a 142 metre-long trestle. Sections of the original trestle are still standing and the original grade is still passable and worth exploring.

144.0   Frame trestle #2.)(110x15

144.68 Rock oven
A small rock oven used to bake bread for the crews building the railway can be found just down and off to the south (left) of the railbed.

145.5   Frame trestle #1.)(78x15

145.6   End of Myra Canyon
A rock barricade prevents motor vehicles from entering the canyon. Parking is limited and turning around can be difficult for larger vehicles.

145.8   Parking
One of the larger limited parking areas on this side of Myra Canyon.

146.5   Ruth Station   ꜜ1247 ⛺ ⁞ 🚴0.2
Originally named Kelowna, but because of confusion with the community of Kelowna, it was renamed Ruth after Andrew McCulloch's younger daughter. The station house is still standing but not for much longer, as it is showing the ravages of time and vandalism. Far below in the valley, Kelowna can be seen through the trees. There are many picturesque viewpoints along this stretch and photo opportunities you will not want to miss.

148.8   Little White Forest Service Road ꜛ
Becomes June Springs Road toward Kelowna.

151.9   Crawford Hiking Trail 🚶 🏕
A staircase comes up from Kelowna. Just down the stairs is a small wilderness campsite with benches and a pond. The trail continues down to Crawford Estates in Kelowna. A second trail branches off to Little White Forest Service Road. The Crawford Hiking Trail follows on the KVR to km 154.8.

155.2   Bellevue Creek)(238 ꜛ 🚶 Δ ꜝ
The Crawford Hiking Trail diverts south and continues to the summit of Little White Mountain. A short distance up the trail is a wilderness campsite. The Bellevue Creek trestle was also upgraded in the 1930s from a frame trestle to steel plate girder spans on steel towers.

155.7   Water tower 🛆
Square concrete blocks placed in an octagonal shape mark the place where the water tower stood.

8

Kettle Valley Railway - Carmi Subdivision
km 163.5 - km 200.8

N

157.5 Lorna Station ⏉1230 🚂 ⑃ 🚲0.3

Lorna was named after the youngest daughter of J. J. Warren, president of the KVR. Hidden in the alders is the foundation of the station house. Very little evidence is visible from the railbed and it is very easy to miss Lorna Station.

159.1 Gillard Creek

The trestle over Gillard Creek has been bypassed using a large fill. The original trestle, minus the top deck, still stands next to the fill.

159.4 Bypass reconnects to old grade.

159.9 Chute Lake Road—Gillard Creek Forest Service Road ⏉

This road leads down into the valley to intersect with Lakeshore Road in Okanagan Mission.

165.5 Pine Beetle Control Area—Lebanon Lake ⏉

A large area was deforested due to an infestation of the mountain pine beetle. The area was reforested with new seedlings in 1992.

170.3 Chute Lake wye. Y

171.4 Chute Lake Station ⏉1191 🚂 ⏉ ⑃ 🛆 🏠 ⏀ ⑃ ⑃ 🚲2.0

Chute Lake Station was named after the lake of the same name. The name Chute Lake came from the creek that resembled a chute or waterfall in its rapid descent to Okanagan Lake. On July 15, 1915, two months after the official opening of the Midway to Merritt line, a steam locomotive with a load of 530 Penticton residents climbed up to Chute Lake for a day picnic. It has been said that the Penticton residents very much enjoyed this new railway.

One can see how the rugged beauty of Chute Lake made this a choice spot for visiting back in 1915 and with very little changed, many still find their way up for a visit. Located at Chute Lake today is Chute Lake Resort, owned and operated by Gary and Doreen Reed. The octagonal-shaped foundation of the water tower can be found in the picnic area. Some of the original red KVR buildings are still in use on the property.

Chute Lake Resort is open year round. The facility offers picnicking, a playground, fishing (the lake is stocked with rainbow trout), boating and canoeing (rentals available), camping, a bathhouse, laundry, six rustic log cabins (each equipped with a fridge, wood-burning stove and kitchen supplies), and a lodge with eight sleeping rooms and a large dining area complete with pool table, an old jukebox and antique decor with many KVR artifacts and pictures.

171.6 Chute Creek.)(18

171.7 Elinor Lake Forest Service Road ⏉ 🛆 ⏉B

A primitive campground is found on the southeast corner of Chute Lake. After leaving Chute Lake, the KVR crosses many small wooden bridges and trestles spanning small creeks. The railbed from Chute Lake to Pen-

Concrete barricade blocking the tunnel exit of Adra Tunnel, km 183.8.

Rock ovens, km 187.1. Ovens such as this one enabled the KVR construction crews to enjoy fresh baked goods.

ticton is downhill allowing you to cruise at a pleasant 13 to 14 km/ hour. Unfortunately, the KVR is also being used by logging trucks and can be a little bumpy in spots with loose gravel and washboard.

TIP: Deflating tires to around 15 psi gives you a better ride and more control as you cruise over the rough Texas pea gravel and loose sand that is encountered on this downhill stretch.

171.9   Chute Creek.)(9

172.0   Chute Creek.)(14

172.1   Chute Creek.)(14

172.2   Chute Creek.)(14

172.3   Chute Creek.)(14

174.1   Access road to Chute Lake Road. �

177.1   Cattle guard.

180.8   Elinor Lake Forest Service Road—North Fork Smethurst Road ⼂
Just before this intersection you cross over a cattle guard. To the east is Elinor Lake Forest Service Road, which follows Robinson Creek to Naramata Lake (3.6 km), Elinor Lake (4.7 km) and Chute Lake (8 km). To the west is North Fork Smethurst Road, which switchbacks down 100 metres in 1.5 kilometres to again intersect with the KVR at the middle segment of the giant loops at km 186.5.

181.9   Adra Station |981 🚂 💺 ⼂ 🚲2.1
Adra Station was located just before the switchbacks that McCulloch used to avoid a grade of 4.5% that would have been required for the descent from Chute Lake to Penticton, an elevation drop of 850 metres over 24 kilometres. Instead, a grade of 2.2% was used with two giant loops. The line doubled back on itself through a spiral tunnel just past Adra, and doubled back again in a second giant loop just past Glenfir Station. The beautiful view from this location, overlooking Okanagan Lake and Summerland, was reminiscent of the Spanish seaport of Adra and Adra Station was appropriately named after it. The water tower and station foundations, complete with sidewalk, remain at this site.

183.1   Adra Tunnel Bypass Trail ⼂➜
This 150 metre-long single track bypasses the collapsed Adra Tunnel and rejoins the railbed at km 184.4.

183.3   Adra Tunnel (The Big Tunnel)   ◼489
This spiral tunnel is the longest tunnel on the KVR. Safe travel through the tunnel can not be guaranteed as the ceiling and walls have given way on the outside of the curve near the lower entrance and there can be over a foot of water at the lower end. In 1992 the entrances of the

Steam locomotive emerges from the "Little Tunnel" at km 196.3 of the Carmi Subdivision. (Penticton Museum)

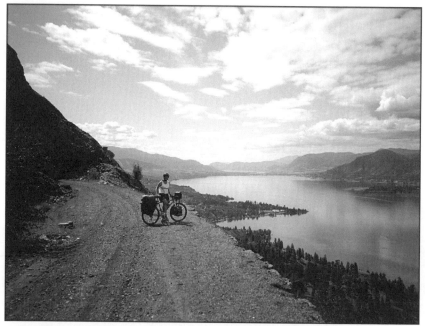

Cycling this part of the Kettle Valley Railway is becoming increasingly popular and why not with such incredible scenery? Looking back at the 48 metre-long "Little Tunnel."

tunnel were partially blocked with walls of cement blocks. A short trail, 140 metres before the tunnel entrance, bypasses the tunnel and reconnects with the railbed just past the exit of the tunnel.

During the building of the KVR many hazards were encountered. One hazard in particular was rattlesnakes. During the rock blasting above Naramata, rattlesnakes were jarred out of their rock hiding places resulting in more than one worker suffering the bite of an angry rattler.

183.8 Tunnel exit

Owing to the heavy grades when descending from Chute Lake to Penticton, brakemen were to stand ready at the brakes. Brake wheels of the freight cars could only be turned from atop the cars, thus requiring brakemen to ride standing atop the freight cars. Such a task was exceedingly risky and more than one brakeman lost his life when the train unexpectedly lurched or stopped.

183.9 South Fork Smethurst Road ↥

Following this road southward, you cross the KVR at km 200.9 to intersect with Naramata Road. Locals prefer to take the heart pumping scramble up this 4x4 road from km 200.9, rather then endure dragging out the ascent on loose sand and gravel switchbacking up the KVR. Going up, this road leads over the top of the tunnel. Many cyclists have gotten lost mistaking this road for the trail to the other end of the tunnel.

184.4 Adra Tunnel Bypass Trail ⇤

The trail joins the railbed 550 metres from the exit of Adra Tunnel.

186.3 Rock ovens

The two smaller rock ovens are up the trail to the east (right). The first one has collapsed and is on the right about 10 metres from the railbed. The second is at 20 metres and is in good shape.

186.5 Elinor Lake Forest Service Road—North Fork Smethurst Road ↥

This road first crossed the railbed farther up the hill, just prior to Adra Station at km 180.8. 4.6 kilometres south along this road connects you to the South Fork Smethurst Road. Turning south on Smethurst Road and travelling another 0.6 kilometres reconnects you with the KVR at km 200.9. Smethurst Road then continues another 0.8 kilometres to connect with Naramata Road.

187.1 Rock ovens

The rock ovens were constructed by Scandinavian railway workers for baking bread and other goods for the men working on the KVR.

The trail to the rock ovens is a faint 4x4 path on the east (right) side, that leads you up a steep climb to the rock ovens. Follow the path for a couple of hundred metres, keeping a watch on your left (close to Trust Creek) for the igloo (beehive) shaped rock ovens. One oven has collapsed, but the second is still intact. From the trail, the ovens appear as a rockpile covered with pine needles and moss, and are hidden back in a pine grove. They can be difficult to find with such good camouflage.

188.1 High tension wires.

192.0 Glenfir Station |788 🚃 ⸽ 🚴2.2

This station was named after a large grove of fir trees that were growing beside the railway. A gravel fill marks the site of the Glenfir Station.

192.1 Chute Lake Road

The apex of the switchback meets the road to Chute Lake.

196.3 Little Tunnel ◼48

The views along this section are unsurpassed as the KVR winds its way down the side of Okanagan Mountain and out of the Okanagan Highlands. Looking down into the valley you can see Okanagan Lake, Summerland, Naramata, Penticton and even as far as Skaha Lake.

Okanagan Lake, 340 metres below this point, is 128 kilometres long and 274 metres deep, and has been noted as a lake of much mystery and folklore. It is known as the home of the fearless lake monster "Ogopogo." This lake monster was originally identified by the Indians as N'ha-a-itk. His home was believed to be a cave at Squally Point at the big bend in the lake. New settlers were warned by the Indians not to go on the lake alone or near his cave, as the monster could rise out of the waves to claim a life. Animals were regularly sacrificed by being thrown overboard in an attempt to calm the beast. Today, people still look out onto Okanagan Lake and wonder if they will catch a glimpse of the sea serpent from the past.

Path overlooking Okanagan Lake. If you look closely, you may see the Ogopogo Monster, km. 195.0. Photo: Robbin McKinney.

198.7   Bench overlooking Okanagan Lake.

200.2   Another bench.

200.9   Smethurst Road (Naramata Creek Road) ⌅
Smethurst Road intersects the KVR at this point, then continues 1.6 kilometres to connect with Naramata Road. The North and South Fork Smethurst roads intersected the KVR at kms 186.5, 183.9 and 180.8.

201.2   Naramata Creek ⋇
The trestle is missing across Naramata Creek, but it is not difficult to cross the creek through the small gully. In the next 0.6 kilometres, trestles are also missing across Arawana Creek and another small creek. This requires you to climb in and out of one steep gulch and a second smaller one to cross each of these creeks. If conditions are wet these gullies are a mud bath.

201.4   Arawana Creek. 🯄 ⋇

202.2   Arawana Station ¦566 🚂 👤 ⌇ 🚲1.8
This was originally named Naramata because of its proximity to the community of Naramata, but confusion between the two locations resulted in a name change. Arawana was named after a song popular at the time, "Aeeah Wannah." The water tower foundation marks the site of Arawana Station. Some of the red KVR buildings have been moved farther down the railway and are being used as a shed and an outhouse.

202.4   Arawana Road—Arawana Creek Forest Service Road. ⌅ ⌹

**⌹ Lang Vineyards (2493 Gammon Road, 496-5987)
Turn down Arawana Road then left on Gammon.**

205.3   Gravel pit
The right-of-way becomes a little less distinct and less travelled. Sections can be quite rough and bouncy with large rocks, black sand and a disturbed trail from use by horses.

206.9   Sutherland Road ⌅
The sign with 467 on it is a benchmark indicating an elevation of 467 metres.

207.7   Poplar Grove Station ¦461 🚂 ⌅ 🚲1.6
The intersection of Riddle Road marks Poplar Grove Station.

208.4   Naramata Road ⌅ ⌹ ⌇→
The railway crosses to the other side of Naramata Road. This section is bordered by some of the orchards that have made the Okanagan Valley famous. Unfortunately, parts of the right-of-way have been leased to the adjacent orchardists by the city of Penticton and continuing to follow the railway past this point will cause you to trespass. Detour on

GIANTS HEAD ▲

🏕 15.3

West Summerland

97

11.7

🏕 11.3

Winslow

10.5

N

9.8

9.2

Okanagan

Lake

MOUNT ▲ NKWALA

Kettle Valley Railway

Carmi Subdivision
km 200.4 - km 215

Princeton Subdivision
km 0.0 - km 16.3

Osoyoos Subdivision
km 0.0 - km 5.5

5.1

4.6

4.0

2.9

2.4

97

Penticton

Shingle   Creek

0.8

0.0

0.4

1.6

South Yard

1.3

0   1   2   3   4 km

0   1   2   3 miles

Indian

🏕 3.4

3.6

97

Skaha   Creek

Reserve

Skaha

Lake

201.2

201.4

Arawana Creek

🏕 202.2   Arawana

202.4

NARAMATA ROAD

205.3 Creek

Turnbull

Four Mile Point

Spring Creek

206.9

Poplar Grove

Three Mile Point

Johnson

Strutt Creek

🏕 207.7

208.4

209.0

209.6   209.4

210.0

210.5

Randolt Cr.

212.3

213.4

Penticton Creek

214.1

Penticton (South)

🏕 215.0

Ellis   Creek

MAIN ST

SKAHA LAKE RD

LAKESIDE RD

9

Naramata Road south (left) to McMillan Avenue, turn west (right) on McMillan to Upper Bench Road, turn north (right) on Upper Bench Road. Stay on Upper Bench by turning north (right) as Upper Bench turns onto Munson Avenue. Upper Bench will then turn west (left) on Corbishley, which in turn will become Lower Bench Road as it turns south (left). This will take you past Lakeview Cemetery where Andrew McCulloch is buried. The railbed runs along the north and west boundaries of the cemetery. Follow south on Lower Bench, which will turn west (right) on Vancouver Avenue. The KVR can be picked up south (left) as it crosses Vancouver Avenue just opposite Vancouver Place.

�X Hillside Cellars (1350 Naramata Road, 493-4424)

209.0   Davenport Road. �X

209.4   Lochore Road �X

There are no current plans to restore the KVR corridor from Lochore Road to Penticton. Some sections on the bank have actually fallen into Okanagan Lake; thus, the right-of-way is no longer there to be reclaimed. The connecting corridor will use the roadways instead. Much of the right-of-way has also been lost to the orchards.

209.6   Randolf Creek ⅄

Evidence of the right-of-way before Randolf Creek has been removed by the adjacent landowner. The trestle over this rather deep gorge is also missing. Along the top of this gorge is a small trail that winds down and back up the other side only to again become lost in the orchards. Detouring is recommended from Naramata Road (km 208.4).

210.0   Carder Road—Orchard ⍭

Across this road the KVR again disappears into an orchard. Detour by following Cardinal Road south and turn right (west) on Corbishley, which curves left (south) to become Lower Bench Road. Turn right (west) into Lakeview Cemetery and follow the road down to the KVR grade.

210.5   Lakeview Cemetery

On December 13, 1945, Andrew McCulloch passed away. He was buried in Lakeview Cemetery overlooking the railway that was such an important part of his life. His grave site can be found in Section D, the first section directly to the right of the main entrance and below the fire hydrant.

Although the KVR can be found between the cemetery and the top of the bench overlooking Okanagan Lake, it is not advised to follow this stretch. Chain link fences have been erected for safety reasons, and bypassing them requires half hanging over the cliff looking down to Okanagan Lake below. These benches are remnants of a beach consisting of glacial debris and can be quite unstable, giving way in slides. It was upon this bench on November 30, 1949, that train #12 was dumped down the side of the bench when it gave way. Irrigation of the orchards along these benches is also increasing the benches instability.

Two kilometres farther along Lower Bench Road, the KVR can be picked up again where Lower Bench Road turns into Vancouver Avenue.

212.3   Vancouver Avenue ⍭ ⍭ ⍭←

The City of Penticton in conjunction with the Rotary Club have developed the KVR right-of-way as a multi-use walking/biking trail from Vancouver Avenue through to Main Street.

Plans are underway to have a trail that follows the KVR right-of-way from the end of Vancouver Place, north for a few hundred metres to a viewpoint. The railbed will then be officially blocked at this point to further travel up the bank toward Poplar Grove.

A memorial was erected in Penticton's Gyro Park in 1959 to honour Andrew McCulloch. Gyro Park can be found by following Vancouver Avenue west, over Penticton Creek to Lakeshore Drive. Gyro Park is located on the corner of Main Street and Lakeshore Drive.

212.4   Townley Street. ⍭

212.6   Westminster Avenue. ⍭

212.8   Nanaimo Avenue. ⍭

213.3   Pickering Street ⍭

Just before Pickering Street the pathway departs the original railbed to detour around a large apartment complex built on the railbed. The pathway reconnects with the original railbed at the bridge.

213.4 Penticton Creek—Government Street)(₁₅ ⸸

This railway deck plate girder span has been converted to a pedestion bridge over Penticton Creek.

213.5 Eckhardt Avenue East. ⸸

213.7 Gahan Avenue—Pentiction Secondary School sports grounds ⸸

After crossing Gahan Avenue the pathway zig-zags across the sports field, whereas the railbed had cut diagonally across the field.

213.9 Jermyn Avenue. ⸸

214.1 Edmonton Avenue—Main Street ⸸ ⊤ ⌂ ⸻ ⸻ ⸻ ⊙

The VV&E was more than just a paper railway before it fell into the hands of J. J. Hill. In 1898, with the dream of being the coast-to-Kootenay railway, a grade was constructed from the government wharf on Okanagan Lake, south toward Skaha Lake and down the Okanagan Valley toward Midway. In less than a year the dream would fizzle with no more than a partially completed railbed between the two lakes. Today, the railbed lies under Front Street and generally follows parallel and just west of Main Street toward Skaha Lake.

⊤ Cartier Wines (2210 Main Street, 492-0621)

Penticton Museum (785 Main Street, 490-2451)

North on main is downtown Penticton where the majority of bike shops are found. Also two blocks north is the Penticton Musem.

An interesting side trip is to the Kettle Valley Station Restaurant and Pub, which has many KVR artifacts in its decor. This restaurant can be found adjacent to the Ramada Courtyard Inn at 1050 Eckhardt Avenue West, which intersects Main Street just north of the museum.

214.4 Calgary Avenue. ⸸

214.8 Fairview Avenue ⸸ ¦→

To continue on to the Princeton or Osoyoos subdivisions, a detour is required here. The Okanagan River Channel Bridge at km 0.7 was removed by the CPR in 1996. To detour follow Fairview Avenue across Highway #97 (Channel Parkway) and the Okanagan River Channel. Just after the bridge connects with the Jaycees bike path. North 800 metres, the path connects with the Princeton Subdivision. South, the path parallels the Osoyoos Subdivision.

*Arrival of the first passenger train from Merritt at Penticton Station, May 31, 1915.
(Penticton Museum)*

215.0 Penticton Station |341| 🚍 🏫 ⌇ Υ

Penticton was the selected location for the KVR headquarters where a station, roundhouse and shop facilities were located. Many "helper" engines also resided here to assist trains up the 2.2% grade out of the Okanagan Valley. The original Penticton Station was located on Okanagan Lake, reached by a short spur from the main railway yard. This site was conveniently situated between the KVR trains and the CPR lake boats. The station site was changed in 1941 after passenger service on Okanagan Lake was discontinued, and a new station was then built at the railway yard.

The Penticton Station of 1941 can still be found on Hastings Avenue. It is now called the Kinsmen Station, housing the Kinsmen Club of Penticton, the Kanettes and the Jaycees.

OSOYOOS SUBDIVISION
Penticton to Osoyoos, 58.1 kilometres

The section of the Kettle Valley Railway from Penticton to Osoyoos became known as the Osoyoos Subdivision. This subdivision encompasses 58 kilometres through the best of the Okanagan, including orchards and vineyards, sandy beaches and warm lakes, the bird and wildlife sanctuary of Vaseux Lake, and south of Oliver, Canada's only true desert. Much of this area is fairly well inhabited, and the railbed at times can be difficult to follow. Successful efforts are being made to preserve the right-of-way through this area, but for now a fair bit of detouring off the railway is required. This unfortunately necessitates you to leave the relatively flat grade of the railbed to tackle the heavier grades of the highway. However, this detouring is not a totally disappointing feature as you do not find too many fruit stands on the KVR!

You start your journey by leaving the Penticton Station and following the railbed west to the Jaycees Bike Path. The KVR grade past the bike path to km 7.1 lies within the boundaries of the Penticton Indian Reserve. A detour is easily found by following the bike path to Skaha Lake, then taking the highway along the west side of the lake. The highway entails a wicked climb, especially in the Okanagan's summer heat, but you can then coast into Okanagan Falls for a dip in Skaha Lake, enjoy an ice cream at one of the many shops, or stay for a day or two in the town.

The railbed can be explored past Okanagan Falls, and along the west side of Vaseux Lake, but your exploration ends short because of a missing trestle. To continue your journey to Osoyoos, you return to Okanagan Falls and follow Oliver Ranch Road. This road takes you up into some beautiful orchards and vineyards. The Oliver Ranch Road then reconnects to the highway at the northeast end of Vaseux Lake. This lake, being a bird and wildlife sanctuary, offers great opportunity for sightings. You may also spot a herd of California bighorn sheep that are frequently seen in the cliffs to the east of this lake.

After following the highway for a short distance, you connect to a cycling trail. The International Bicycling and Hiking Society of Oliver have developed a 17.4 kilometre-long hiking and cycling trail from Highway #93 to Osoyoos Lake. Passing through Oliver, you find the original Oliver Railway Station, which has been converted into the tourist information centre. The full length of this trail is not actually atop the KVR grade, but along the Okanagan River. It ends abruptly at the north end of Osoyoos Lake where you then reaccess the highway and follow it into Osoyoos.

Except for the highway, the grade along this route is relatively flat. The biggest challenge is cycling in the heat of the desert sun. The heat alone can sap your energy just as any challenging uphill climb can. As you look around, you notice the unirrigated land is dry and parched, and don't be surprised if you see a turtle or rattlesnake cross your path! But then the advantage to this desert climate is seen where the irrigation starts. From

Kettle Valley Railway
Osoyoos Subdivision
Penticton to Osoyoos
58.1 km

Kettle Valley Railway – Osoyoos Subdivision Profile

the roadside, you can see an abundance of fruit growing in the orchards. An interesting detour is to visit one of the many vineyards for some wine tasting. The vineyards of this area are known to produce award-winning wines. You also won't want to pass up the chance to stop for some cherry cider at one of the numerous fruit stands that are found throughout this valley, or stop and pick some fruit at a U-pick orchard.

Well, if you were previously uncertain, I'm sure you are now convinced that this subdivision through the Okanagan Valley is well worth exploring. Even though the 58 kilometres from Penticton to Osoyoos can be easily cycled in one day, you may want to take your time to enjoy all this valley has to offer, as many camping and lodging accommodations can be found all along this route. The warm and welcoming people of this valley, not to mention the opportunity of travelling through the beautiful orchards and vineyards, stopping at a fruit stand or winery, experiencing the desert land of sand and scrub, then completing the venture at Osoyoos Lake, give reason enough to cruise the distance. In fact, you may never want to leave ▄▄

km	**Penticton Station** |341| 🚉 💺 📆 Ƴ Λ ⌂ ⌐ 🛢 ‖ 🍴 (🚲

0.0 Penticton was a junction point for the Osoyoos Subdivision. The trains connected to either the Carmi or Princeton subdivisions, or to the Okanagan Lake boats. The construction of this subdivision began with a line from the Penticton Station to a station at Skaha Lake. The section from Penticton Station to Skaha Station was completed in 1920, with the line from Okanagan Falls to Hayes being completed in 1923. The KVR right-of-way is easily followed west from Penticton Station.

The Osoyoos Subdivision mileposts start at km 0.9 along the Princeton Subdivision where the Osoyoos Subdivision connects with it.

0.7 Channel Parkway)(/ Okanagan River Channel ✗27 ⤑

Two railway bridges, one right after the other, cross the Channel Parkway and the Okanagan River Channel. The Okanagan River Channel bridge was removed by CPR in June of 1996. A detour is required to get around the missing bridge. Take Fairview Road south across Channel Parkway and the Okanagan River Channel. After crossing the bridge turn south (right) on the Jaycees bike path.

0.8 "Jaycees" bicycle path

The bike path is the western boundary of the Penticton Indian Reserve. Permission is required to cross the reserve and can be gained by calling the band office. It extends south along the channel's length to Skaha Lake. You must detour from the railway to this bike path, as the railbed to the south becomes impassable with six foot-high barbed wire fences indicating the boundary of the Penticton Indian Reserve. During the building of the KVR the land between km 0.0 and km 7.1 was expropriated from the Penticton Indian Band. The use of this land was granted for as long as railway service was in operation. Now that the line has been abandoned, this land has been reclaimed by its original owners.

Kettle Valley Railway - Osoyoos Subdivision
km 6.5 - 25.9

0.9/0.0 Princeton-Osoyoos Subdivision junction.

0.4   Shingle Creek. ⵋ45

0.7   Green Mountain Road. �熙

1.3   South Yard ⵍ
The South Yard was a busy station in its prime. Trains loaded with
fruit would travel up the Osoyoos line to Penticton. These reefers
stopped at the ice house in the South Yard to be iced that afternoon.
They then continued their journey by rail, or were loaded onto the
Okanagan Lake barge. It was boasted that with this type of transportation fruit could be on market counters within 48 hours.
    The South Yard site lies within the boundaries of the Penticton In-
dian Reserve, and is inaccessible without trespassing. Building foundations, railway platforms and scattered lumber remain at this site.

3.4   Skaha Station ⎮340 🏠 ⵍ ⵘ
Between 1920 and 1931 trains were shuttled the 12 kilometres down
Skaha Lake by barge from Skaha Station to Okanagan Falls. When the
railway along the lake was completed in 1931, the tug and barge service ended. Today there is little evidence of the existence of the station.

3.6   Highway #97 ⵘ
The railbed south of this point is still within the Penticton Indian Reserve. You can detour two ways. One is to follow Highway #97 on the
west side of Skaha Lake to reconnect with the KVR at km 9.2, a detour
of 5.2 kilometres. The second is to turn east on Highway #97 to connect
to South Beach Drive, which then connects you with South Main Street.
South Main Street becomes Lakeside Road and follows the east shore
of Skaha Lake to Okanagan Falls, a detour of 15.2 kilometres. Both routes
entail a steep climb and the hazard of motorized traffic. Highway #97 is
particularly busy with car and truck traffic, but the shoulders are adequate for safe travel. Lakeside Road does not have wide shoulders, but
it also does not have the traffic volume or speed found on Highway
#97, which may provide for a more relaxed ride.

7.1   Penticton Indian Reserve boundary
The railbed south of the reserve boundary has been fairly well trav-
elled, but can only be reached by turning off Highway #97 at Pineview
Drive, then backtracking along the railbed.

8.4   Banbury Green RV Park (tenting welcome) ⵘ Δ ⵏ←
Access this park by taking Pineview Drive from Highway #97. The park
access road crosses the KVR grade. The railbed south to km 16.1 is
easily cycled, except for a few sandy spots, allowing you to really cruise
on this level grade. The scenery is also impressive as you skirt along
the shore of Skaha Lake.

A detour is required here because part of the top deck of this pile trestle has been removed, km 16.1 Skaha Lake.

The section along Skaha Lake is particularly scenic.

Vineyards and Orchards

The Okanagan Valley is blessed with ideal conditions for growing wine grapes, which has led to a wine making history that is decades old. The local wineries have developed a reputation for producing top quality wine, meeting world-class standards. Tours and tastings are offered daily at most wineries we have listed (phone ahead for confirmation).

South Okanagan Valley: Blossom and ripening times

Apricots: April 15 - 30 / June 18 - July 15

Cherries: April 18 - May 10 / July 8 - August 18

Peaches: April 20 - May 10 / July 25 - September 15

Pears: April 28 - May 10 / August 10 and on

Apples: May 1 - May 20 / July 31 and on

Grapes: June 15 - 25 / August 15 and on

MOUNT KEOGAN ▲

Vaseux Lake

26.3

⌂ 27.2

McIntyre

MCINTYRE BLUFF ▲

29.2

Park Rd

Rill

11

97

Gallagher Lake

31.4

Okanagan

97

River

Tugulnuit Lake

Wolfcub

Creek

N

Oliver

⌂ 36.5

37.3

Fairview

Kettle Valley Railway - Osoyoos Subdivision
km 24.6 - 44.5

0   1   2   3   4 km

0   1   2   3 miles

Tinhorn Cr

Rd 8

Creek Rd 11

Hester

Hayes

⌂ 42.0

11.1   Kaleden Station   ¦344 🚋 ⌇ ⌂ ⌶ ⍾ 🛉 🚲

The distance between Penticton and Okanagan Falls was originally linked by barge service. This involved loading the train on and off the Skaha Lake barge, with delayed service in the winter if the lake froze over. In 1931, the CPR upgraded this subdivision with a connecting line along the west shore of Skaha Lake. This was the last work to be done on the Kettle Valley Railway by Andrew McCulloch, as he formally retired January 31, 1933, after 23 years of service.

Kaleden Station was named after the community of Kaleden, which adopted this name in 1909. It was formed from a combination of "Kalos," the Greek word meaning beautiful, and the biblical orchard Eden. The first fruit trees were planted in 1910 and some began bearing fruit in 1913 (apricots). By 1914 apples were being shipped to market.

16.1   Okanagan River ⋇ ⌇→

There is a long pile trestle across the outfall of the Okanagan River at the south end of Skaha Lake. This trestle is blocked and a section of the top deck has been removed, necessitating a detour on a small road just before the trestle. The 0.8 kilometre detour is a short steep climb reconnecting you with Highway #97. Follow the highway for a short distance. Just after tho highway crosses the Okanagan River, it crosses the KVR.

16.9   Highway #93 ⍭

The railbed is marginally passable from here to the missing trestle at Shuttleworth Creek at km 17.7.

17.1   Okanagan Falls Station ¦337 🚋 ⌇ Δ ⌂ ⌂ ⌶ ⍾ 🛉 (🚲

It is here at Okanagan Falls that the Okanagan Indians maintained a year-round village. The rapids and falls of the Okanagan River provided one of the best salmon fishing grounds. The Indians lined the banks to spear fish as they passed by en route to their spawning grounds.

The present dam has disrupted the original series of falls and rapids, which gave Okanagan Falls its name. However, the Okanagan River still offers good fishing, with trout and whitefish throughout the year and large and small mouth bass during the summer.

Although sections of the railbed south of Okanagan Falls can be explored, you must backtrack to Okanagan Falls because of missing bridges. A detour is therefore required at this point. To detour, take Highway #97 through Okanagan Falls to Maple Street and turn south. This street then becomes Oliver Ranch Road. There is a bit of a climb involved, but the great scenery of orchards and vineyards will make up for the extra effort. The Oliver Ranch Road reconnects you to Highway #97 at the north end of Vaseux Lake.

If you wish to further explore the railbed on the west side of Vaseux Lake, head south on Green Lake Road on the west end of Okanagan Falls. Just past Okanagan Falls Provincial Park is a small road that gives access to another road running along the west side of the Okanagan River, intersecting with the KVR at km 19.8. Watch for the raspberries that grow wild along this stretch.

In keeping with rails-to-trails, should we call this sign in Okanagan Falls a bike crossing sign?

The station in Oliver has been beautifully restored and is now an information centre.

Ⲧ **LeComte Estate Winery (Green Lake Road, 497-8267)**
Ⲧ **Wild Goose Vineyard (Sun Valley Way,**
off Oliver Ranch Road, 497-8919)
Ⲧ **Blue Mountain Vineyards and Cellars**
(Oliver Ranch Road, 497-8244)

17.2　Northwood Mill spur Ⲳ

This 2.6 kilometre spur climbs the east hillside at a steep 4% grade to the Northwood lumbermill. The grade runs alongside the road to the mill and is passable though weedy.

17.7　Shuttleworth Creek. Ӿ18

19.6　Okanagan River. Ӿ55

19.8　Vaseux-Bighorn National Wildlife Area

Vaseux Lake was named using the French word "vaseux," meaning muddy or miry. Vaseux Lake Provincial Park encompasses the Vaseux-Bighorn National Wildlife Area, a sanctuary for birds and wildlife. Some birds that can be seen include trumpeter swans and Canada geese that nest there yearly. California bighorn sheep can also be seen on the cliffs across Highway #97 to the east of Vaseux Lake. Sheep crossing signs are posted on the highway to try to avoid mishap.

The intersection of the road along the Okanagan River Channel and the railbed is the northern border of the Vaseux-Bighorn National Wildlife Area. The railway from here is quite weedy around a small rock slide area making travel difficult. One option is to continue to follow the road along the top of the canal to the north end of the lake, then cut across a small flood control dam to the railway. This detour can be difficult. The weeds are about six feet tall at the dam, and there are breaks in the dam that are bridged by three inch-wide beams. It makes for quite a balancing act to get your bike and yourself across without getting wet. But don't worry, the fall is only about two feet. The other option is to reaccess Green Lake Road on your west, head south on Green Lake Road and turn on to the first major road on the left. The end of this road crosses the railbed just prior to some private property at the north end of Vaseux Lake.

22.0　Access road Ⲧ

The railbed along the west shore of Vaseux Lake is a well-travelled one-lane road, although sandy in some spots. You can follow the railbed until the missing bridge at km 26.3. This area of the Okanagan is a land of cactus and rattlesnakes. The landscape is very dry and sandy, and scattered with clumps of cacti and patches of sun-bleached grass.

26.3　Vaseux Lake　Ӿ115

A small road branches off to the right at the terminus of the railbed, but it quickly dwindles out after one kilometre.

12

Hayes
42.0

Tinhorn Cr
Rd B
Hester Cr
Rd 1

Testalinden Cr

Rd B
Okanagan

48.8
Ellis
Rd 22
River

Inkaneep Cr

51.7

N

Osoyoos

97

Lake

3

Osoyoos
58.1

Kettle Valley Railway - Osoyoos Subdivision
km 38.4 - 58.1

0   1   2   3   4 km

0   1   2   3 miles

27.2   McIntyre Station |333 🚂

McIntyre Station was named after Peter McIntyre, one of the "Overlanders" of 1862 who settled at the base of McIntyre Bluff in 1886. McIntyre Bluff is the location of the great ice dam that formed after the last glacier, causing Lake Penticton to back up all the way to Sicamous. Evidence of its great depth can still be seen in the horizontal benches of former beaches all along the Okanagan hillsides. As the ice dam slowly melted, the lake dropped in stages, creating level after level of remnant beach. This scenic bluff is steeped in Indian legends about buffalo and rival Indian bands being driven over its edge. Indian pictographs can be found inscribed on rocks at the base of the cliff.

The McIntyre Station site can be found by taking a short back road from Highway #97. However, no evidence of this station is found. The right-of-way is weedy, rough and barely passable to km 29.2.

Ŧ Brights Wines (North Highway #97, 498-4981)
Ŧ Inkameep Vineyards (Tuculnuit Road, 498-3552)

28.4   Irrigation canal. ⅀55

29.2   Okanagan River. ⅀66

31.4   Highway #97 Ŧ

You can access the bicycling/hiking trail or the KVR railbed just past the McAlpine Bridge on Highway #97, which crosses the Okanagan River. As part of an envisioned International Hike and Bike Corridor from Brewster, Washington to Vernon, B.C., the International Bicycling and Hiking Society has already developed 17.4 kilometres from McAlpine Bridge to the north shore of Osoyoos Lake.

The trail has not utilized the true KVR right-of-way, but is located slightly to the east of the railbed. Because the railbed had been mostly claimed by bordering landowners, the corridor of the Old River Road was used. This narrow road has been turned into a multi-use trail that follows along the Okanagan River Channel.

33.9   Park Rill. ⅀36

36.5   Oliver Station |297 🚂 ⫯ ⛺ 🏛 🪑 🚻 🍴 (☂0.1

The original KVR Station at Oliver has been restored and designated an historic site. The building now houses the Oliver Tourist Infocentre and the International Bicycling and Hiking Society.

The true railbed around Oliver is at times difficult to follow. The KVR right-of-way at Oliver Station is actually to the west side of the station/infocentre in the middle of the parking lot. If you wish to explore the railbed, follow 93 Street across 348 Avenue from the parking lot. It then disguises itself as an alley. As you cross 346 Avenue the right-of-way follows along the west side of 91 Street. The remaining

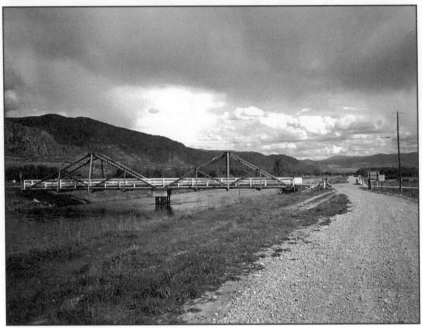

The International Bicycling and Hiking Society has established an excellent trail that follows beside the Okanagan River Channel, km 48.8.

Osoyoos Station, km 58.1, has been restored and now houses the Osoyoos Lake Sailing Club.

KVR to Osoyoos is barely passable at best. Where the railbed is used as an access road to fields, it can be in good riding condition. However, many sections have been fenced and have seen little traffic resulting in an overgrowth of tall weeds, bushes and trees. To continue your journey to Osoyoos, follow atop the bicycling and hiking trail.

▰▰▰ Oliver Museum ▰▰▰
(#9728-356 Avenue, 498-4027)

41.1 Tinhorn Creek. ⊁26

41.7 Wye. Y

42.0 Hayes Station |289 🚋 ⊺ 🚲0.1

The purpose of this branch line was for the transportation of fruit. No formal passenger service ever operated on the Osoyoos Subdivision, although passengers were permitted to ride in the freight train caboose. The stations instead served the freight from the fruit packing houses and a small number of sawmills along the route. At Hayes Station you can still find the remains of an old fruit packing plant. This can be reached from the bike path by heading west on No. 8 Road.

Ⲧ **Gehringer Brothers (No. 8 Road, detour 2.1 km, 498-3537)**
Ⲧ **Divino Estate Winery (No. 8 Road, detour 2.1 km, 498-2784)**
Ⲧ **Okanagan Vineyards (No. 11 Road, detour 1.8 km, 498-6663)**

43.3 Fruit warehouse spur. Y

48.8 Ellis Station |281 🚋 ⊺ ⚘ ⊩ 🚲

Ellis Station was situated at the south end of Deadman Lake. As with the other small stations in this subdivision, there is not much evidence of its existence. What can be found at this site is the Oliver Kiwanis Desert Oasis Picnic Park. To reach this park, take No. 22 Road up to the highway, then turn north back to No. 21 Road.

Number 22 Road crosses the Okanagan River Channel and intersects the bike trail. At this intersection, there is a small parking area and a covered information pavilion. The bike trail continues past this point for only a short distance, then ends abruptly at the north end of Osoyoos Lake. You cannot access the highway or railbed from this point but must return to No. 22 Road. Following up No. 22 Road you can see the railbed just prior to Highway #97. You can either follow the highway into Osoyoos, or follow the railbed from No. 22 Road to Willow Beach Trailer Park. The right-of-way is passable except for a couple of gates.

51.7   Willow Beach Trailer Park ⵏ

Just past the trailer park the railbed is disrupted, overgrown and marginally passable. Although the majority of the right-of-way is in good shape, from here to Osoyoos Station it has been subdivided and parcels have been sold to home builders and adjacent landowners. It's disheartening to be cycling lazily along this beautiful orchard-lined path and run into a new house blocking further progress. As the KVR is divided up from the trailer park to Osoyoos, take the trailer park access road to Highway #97, then follow the highway into Osoyoos.

55.1   Fruit warehouse spur. ⎪⁄

57.3   Osoyoos wye. Υ

58.1   Osoyoos Station i281🚃 ⎪ ⎪⁄ Ⅹ ⌂ ᴨ ⫯ ⫯⫯ ⬤ (

There is little evidence of the KVR railway in Osoyoos, the terminal point of this line. The Osoyoos Station can still be found beside Lions Centennial Park. It has been restored and now houses the Osoyoos Lake Sailing Club.

🚂 Osoyoos Museum 🚂
(Lions Centennial Park)

With the exception of a few industrial spurs, the completion of the Osoyoos Subdivision from Hayes to Osoyoos in 1944 was the last piece of trackage built on the Kettle Valley Railway. When the line from Hayes farther south into orchard country was extended, an increase in the amount of fruit being transported on the KVR resulted.

Even today, fruit is part of the very existence of this valley. The city of Osoyoos boasts of having the earliest fruit season in the valley, with crops of cherries, plums, pears, apples and all kinds of vegetables. You can even find a banana farm!

58.6   End of track.

Myra Canyon, Trestle #4, Carmi Subdivision, km 141.89.

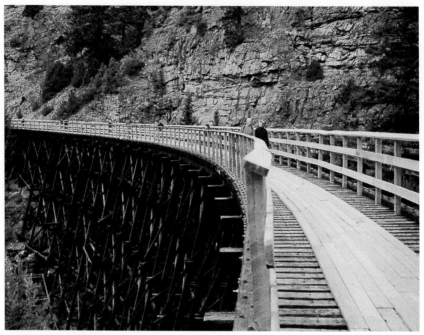

Myra Canyon, Trestle #11, Carmi Subdivision, km 138.22.

Looking across Myra Canyon at Trestle #4, Carmi Subdivision, km 141.89.

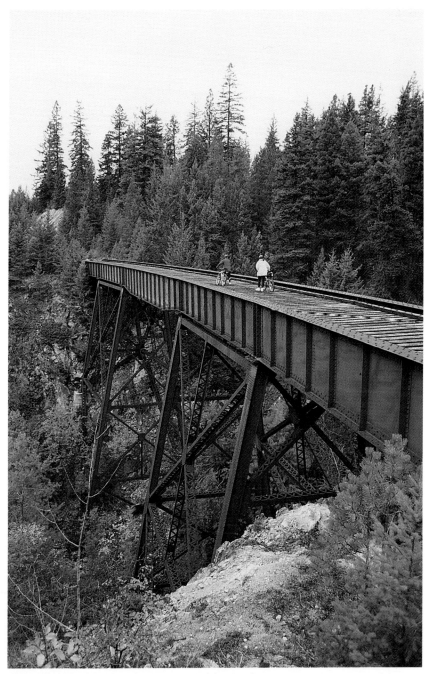

Crossing Spukunne Creek Bridge, Princeton Subdivision, km 81.0.

Railway maintenance shed still stands at the south entrance of Fisherman Tunnel, km 122.9, Columbia & Western Railway.

1924 Shay Locomotive building steam in preparation for hauling the Kettle Valley Steam Railway train up Prairie Valley, km 15.3, Princeton Subdivision.

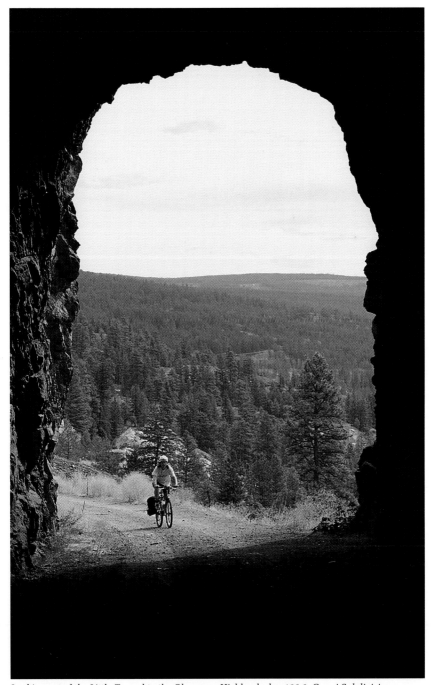

Looking out of the Little Tunnel to the Okanagan Highlands, km 196.3, Carmi Subdivision.

Portal of Tunnel, km 23.6, Columbia & Western.

Participants of the 1996 Kettle Valley Railway Mountain Bike Tour exiting the Little Tunnel, km 196.3, Carmi Subdivision.

The only remaining water tower on the KVR. This tower is unique in that it had two spouts to service both the KVR and VV&E at Brookmere Station, km 174.9 Princeton Subdivision.

A small tuscan red shed built into the hillside at Coykendahl Station, km 28.7, Columbia & Western Railway.

One of the many pile trestles crossing Otter Creek, km 152.1, Princeton Subdivision.

PRINCETON SUBDIVISION
Penticton to Brookmere, 174.9 kilometres

The section of the Kettle Valley Railway between Penticton and Brookmere was known as the Princeton Subdivision. This subdivision offers 174.9 kilometres of recreational riding into some unspoiled backcountry that has changed little since the turn of the century. The railbed is well travelled, enabling you to really push your endurance to go the distance. Along this route, as you cycle into the past, you experience the peaceful and scenic surroundings of this country. It is a truly a fascinating place to explore.

Leaving Penticton to begin your venture, you must pedal your fat tires up and out of the Okanagan Valley. The railbed is in great condition, and don't worry too much about the uphill grade. Remember, you are still on a railway. Views from this upper bench are impressive. You can stop to rest as you look down into the valley toward Okanagan Lake and the surrounding communities. Once back on your bike, you have to stop short of the Trout Creek bridge, 73 metres high and 76 metres long. It was constructed by McCulloch to cross this deep canyon to reach Summerland. Don't be surprised if your adrenalin surges as you glance down between the open ties to the gaping chasm below your feet. It is the highest bridge on the KVR.

Past the bridge, the railbed is in good condition—for a train. The tracks are still in place for the next 16 kilometres, where the Kettle Valley Steam Railway makes regular trips along Prairie Valley. There is no side path for cyclists, so unless you want your brain scrambled, you have to either walk the rails, cycle the detour road or take the train. You can reaccess the gravel railbed at Faulder. From there, cruise the gentle but steady uphill grade along the steep-walled Trout Creek Valley.

The summit of the Princeton Subdivision is reached at Osprey Lake, a nice place to camp for the night. For the next 30 kilometres, you wind your way out of the Hayes Creek Valley. However, even with the downhill grade of the railbed, the valley bottom falls at a steeper grade leaving you high on the side of the bordering hills. This offers some impressive views of the lakes and ranchland below.

As you reach Jura, you share a short length of the trail with some local cows. For this reason, be sure to watch for any hazards that may have dropped on the trail—if you know what I mean. Once out of the barnyard, you descend by cruising along the loops of the KVR across the open rangeland on the hills above Princeton. Upon reaching the Princeton Station site, you will have put 113.4 kilometres between you and Penticton. The city of Princeton offers most services, and makes a nice break in the journey, be it for lunch or the night. You can also spend the day exploring the Copper Mountain Subdivision of the KVR. This branch line runs from Princeton to the Copper Mountain Mine.

Continuing on the Princeton Subdivision, the railbed is still well-travelled and easily cycled. As you pedal up the gentle grade, you find yourself in the steep-walled Tulameen River Valley. The trail follows along the winding corridor carved by the clear waters of the Tulameen River, an interesting river that at one point can be racing and roaring over huge boulders and then at the next be quietly lapping a sandy beach. Wildlife abound in this area, and it is not uncommon to see a group of deer or even a black bear picnicking in the berry patches.

Twenty kilometres down the trail from Princeton you come across the near ghost town of Coalmont and the site of Granite City. Don't be in too much of a hurry. You'll want to stop and explore the area and visit the historic Coalmont Hotel. This hotel was built in 1912, and has recently been completely restored. Coalmont can be an overnight stop or just a refueling break in either the hotel dining room or pub.

Once back on the railbed, continue to pedal the easy grade along the river valley, winding your way through the green forests. Only six kilometres from Coalmont, you pass the entrance to Otter Lake Provincial Park, which offers great camping facilities. Past Otter Lake you follow Otter Creek to the town of Brookmere. This small town sits quietly in the pines, 35 kilometres down the railbed from Otter Lake. No services exist at Brookmere—just a few remaining local residents and some KVR artifacts, such as the water tower and a wooden caboose, reminding you that this town was once a bustling railway centre.

You can hardly deny the feeling you get when cycling this section. With its remote stretches of backcountry leading you deep into the wilderness, there are times where you, your bike and the trail seem to merge into one, and all that surrounds you is peace and solitude. Even when encountering more populated areas, the laidback pace and local lifestyle of this region make you feel right at home on your three-to-four day cycle of the Princeton Subdivision of the Kettle Valley Railway ▄▄

Kettle Valley Railway – Princeton Subdivision Profile

From the upper bench, km 6.0, some scenic views of the Okanagan Valley await you.

The Kettle Valley Steam Railway may soon be running across the tracks of the famous Trout Creek bridge to re-create an incredible piece of history, km 11.7.

km   **Penticton Station** |341 🚋 ▮) Υ Λ ⌂ ⌐ (▮ ⚓1.1
0.0

From Penticton Station to West Summerland Station the grade of the railway varies more than any other section. Although the average is a comfortable 1.1% uphill grade, it does vary from 0.0% to 2.2%.

0.7   Channel Parkway)(/ Okanagan River Channel ⋊27 |→

Two railway bridges, one right after the other, cross the Channel Parkway and the Okanagan River Channel. The Okanagan River Channel bridge was removed by CPR in June of 1996. A detour is required to get around the missing bridge. Take Fairview Road south across Channel Parkway and the Okanagan River Channel. After crossing the bridge turn north (right) on the Jaycees bike path. Eight hundred metres down the path turn west (left) on to the KVR at km 0.8.

0.8   "Jaycees" bicycle path |←

The bike path is the western boundary of the Penticton Indian Reserve. Permission is required to cross the reserve and can be gained by calling the band office.

0.9   Osoyoos Subdivision junction Υ

The railway splits, the south line heading for Skaha Station on the Osoyoos Subdivision, and the northwest line heading for West Summerland Station on the Princeton Subdivision.

2.4   Entering West Bench—leaving Penticton Indian Reserve

Alternating between deep cuts and large fills over coulees, the KVR climbs steadily to mount the bench. As the bench is attained, the KVR bisects the community of West Bench, passing through orchards and behind private residences.

2.9   Right-of-way passes under Sunglo Drive.

4.0   Right-of-way passes under Newton Road.

4.6   Right-of-way passes under Hyslop Road.

5.1   Pine Hills Golf and Country Club Road ⅄

As you leave West Bench, the railway hugs the hillside as it climbs up along Sage Mesa. The views down the Okanagan Valley are spectacular, with views of Okanagan Lake and Penticton to the south and Naramata to the north. The views improve as the railway continues its uphill climb on an excellent hard-packed lane toward West Summerland.

9.2   The KVR hangs high on a rock face overlooking the Okanagan Valley.

9.8   Small access road from West Bench and Research Centre. ⅄
The Research Centre is fenced and locked with no access.

Kettle Valley Railway - Princeton Subdivision
km 16.2 - km 39.8

10.5   Beginning of Winslow siding

Winslow siding is located on a wide upper bench. This is the planned terminus of the Kettle Valley Steam Railway. Plans include a railway station with access to the Agricultural Research Station.

11.1   End of Winslow siding.

11.3   **Winslow Station** ¦*460* 🚂 ⟩ ⚓*1.6*

Winslow Station was named after R. M. Winslow of the provincial department of Agriculture who was primarily responsible for the development of the Dominion Experimental Farm. It was established in 1914 to assist the development of the agricultural industry in the unique environmental conditions of the Okanagan Valley. The name was later changed to the Summerland Agricultural Research Station and borders the KVR at Winslow Station. The research centre has become an international tourist attraction providing tours of the interpretive centre and botanical gardens. Although there is a gated road coming out of the research station here, there is no access to the botanical gardens or research station. The only access is from Highway #97.

11.7   Trout Creek)(*76x73*

Trout Creek was a major obstacle for the KVR as the creek had cut a deep canyon in its plunge to Okanagan Lake. For this reason, bypassing Summerland was a cheaper and shorter route. However, at the insistence of the residents of Summerland who wanted to have the KVR run to their community, McCulloch engineered a 73 metre-high and 76 metre-long deck truss bridge to cross the canyon. The wooden approach trestles were replaced by steel structures and later by fills in 1928. It is the highest of its type in North America.

The tracks are in place from the south end of Trout Creek bridge to Faulder Station.

12.3   Canyon View Road ↑ ¦⇨

With the tracks still in place and an active steam railway operating on them, the best option is to detour from here and reaccess the railbed at Faulder, km 24.9. An even better idea is to take the train from Summerland Station to Prairie Valley Station, then cycle the road to Faulder before reaccessing the railway.

To detour, take Canyon Road east (left) to Lewis Avenue. Turn north (right) on to Lewis Avenue, then east (left) on to Hillborn, north (right) on to Monro and east (left) on to Victoria Road South. This route takes you for the most part alongside the KVR. Just before Victoria Road South intersects with Lenzi Street is the site of West Summerland Station and the main station for the Kettle Valley Steam Railway.

13.0   Lewis Avenue. ↑

13.6   Monro Avenue. ↑

All aboard—the Kettle Valley Steam Railway, West Summerland Station, km 15.3.

Switching ends of the train at Prairie Valley Station for the return trip to West Summerland, km 20.7.

Summerland

NOT TO SCALE

15.3 **West Summerland Station** ∣523 🚂 ▮ 🚆 ⌇ 𝄛 🏛 ⛩🍴🍎 (🚲 1.5

The station is again alive with a real steam engine making regular trips up Prairie Valley. Formed in 1989, the Kettle Valley Heritage Society succeeded in keeping a small piece of KVR alive for generations to come. With a 1924 Shay logging locomotive restored by the B.C Forest Museum at Duncan, the society started passenger service on September 17, 1995. With the help of many volunteers and organizations, the railway will continue to expand, eventually running from Winslow to Faulder. Presently (1997) the train makes regular runs between West Summerland Station and Prairie Station at km 20.7. Construction of new stations at Winslow, West Summerland and Faulder are in the plans. Of the original station, the octagonal water tower foundation can be found beside the tracks 300 metres before the station.

A large log like this one makes a good substitute for a bridge or trestle at Trout Creek, km 37.7.

The trail is frequently broken by trestles and bridges like this one crossing Trout Creek at km 39.7.

Summerland Museum
9521 Wharton Street, 494-9395

The railway leaves the station and starts its climb along the north side of Mount Conkle. Rows of fruit trees carpet the valley bottom as you skirt the southern perimeter of Prairie Valley. Although this section contains those postcard views that the Okanagan is famous for, following it by bike is difficult. Riding between the rails will shake every bolt loose on your bike and there is no edge along the ties on which to ride. For the hard-core cyclist who has to do it all, the only option is to walk your bike along the rails. Of course, this option is only open when the Kettle Valley Steam Railway is not operating.

To detour, continue north up Victoria Road South. Turn west (left) on Dale Meadows Road and follow it for 2.9 kilometres. Turn north (right) on to Lister Avenue, east (left) on to Prairie Valley Road, north (right) on to Doherty Avenue and east (left) on to Bathfield Street, then follow the signs to Faulder. Of course, this detour requires that you climb more than the elevation difference between Faulder and West Summerland in less than three kilometres.

15.6   Lenzi Avenue.

17.4   Gould Avenue.)(

20.6   Summerland Dump Road.

20.7   Prairie Valley Station
This is the current (1997) terminus of the Kettle Valley Steam Railway. The train can be taken to this point or picked up at this point. Future plans of the railway will see it continue to Faulder. From here to Faulder the tracks are still present and are difficult to cycle. Take the Dump Road out to Highway #40 and turn west (left) to Faulder. Distance from station to end of track at Faulder by road is 6.4 kilometres.

23.9   Local access road.

24.9   Faulder Station ¡670 ⚫ 🚂 ⌡ ✗ 🔺1.5
This is the planned western terminus of the Kettle Valley Steam Railway.

25.7   Community of Faulder.

25.9   Both Faulder siding and the tracks end here. ⇐

28.6   Loose sandy railbed.

30.6   Trout Creek Canyon narrows
The KVR squeezes between the roaring rapids of Trout Creek and the vertical canyon walls. Beware of rock slides and rocks on the trail.

Kettle Valley Railway - Princeton Subdivision
km 39.4 - km 61.6

32.5 Crump ⍏

Crump was a flag stop named after a KVR superintendent.

33.0 Twenty Mile Tank. ⍟

33.5 Shallow creek to ford—won't get too wet.

33.6 High tension wires.

37.6 Gravel mounds and ditches

Large mounds of gravel and deep ditches cut across the railbed to prevent vehicle traffic from falling into Trout Creek owing to a missing bridge.

37.7 Trout Creek ⨉58 ⍙ᴮ

This bridge was removed by CPR in 1995. All that remains are the two concrete towers that once held up the three deck plate girder spans. A steep trail on the north side of the railbed leads down to the creek. During low stream levels the creek can be forded. Otherwise, a large log across the creek makes a natural bridge for those with good balance. Located on the west side of the creek is a natural backcountry campsite. The trail is a little less obvious when coming from the other direction, but is just before the gravel mounds and ditches on the west side of the missing bridge.

38.3 Highway #40 ⍏

The KVR enters Kirton Canyon, another narrow steep-walled canyon of Trout Creek. Trout Creek Crossing Forest Service Campground is 100 metres east down the road.

39.2 Cave.

39.7 Trout Creek)(23

Kirton Canyon widens out.

40.4 Access road to Highway #40 ⍏ ⍙

40.5 Kirton Station wye, overgrown with trees.

41.4 Kirton Station |910 ⬤ ⏐ ⍦ ⛵1.1

The name Kirton was derived from the first part of J. Kirkpatrick's name, the KVR's first agent at Penticton, and the last part of the name from Penticton. A wye was built at Kirton, the end of the 2.2% grade from Penticton, for turning helper engines.

The station house has been pushed off its foundation and over the cliff. Not much is visible on the right-of-way except a cement foundation and a cellar foundation at km 41.5.

44.4 Demuth ⬤

This station was formerly called Altamont, but there is very little left to mark the passing of this station.

Missing bridge across Kathleen Creek at km 59.6.

A pile trestle spans the east end of Osprey Lake at km 63.3.

44.9 Private access road to Highway #40 ⟱ ⚑
Demuth Forest Service Campsite is s small semi-open site just off Highway #40 on the shore of Trout Creek.

45.6 O'Hagan Creek.

46.2 Viewpoint
The KVR is high on the north slope of Trout Creek Valley overlooking a pastoral green valley bottom.

47.5 **Thirty Mile Tank.** 🏭

47.6 Tsuh Creek.

48.7 Camp Creek
A very high fill carries the KVR over Camp Creek.

50.2 Access road to Highway #40 ⟱
An old siding to the north reconnects with the main line.

52.1 **Thirsk Station** ⏐1008 🚂 ⏐ 🚲1.0
Named after the Thirsk community in Penticton. Thirsk is a district in England.

52.7 Access road to Highway #40 ⟱ ⚑
Demuth Forest Service Campsite is east on Highway #40 on the shore of Trout Creek.

53.8 Highway #40
Unfortunately, the highway jumps up onto the railgrade for the next 2.3 kilometres. The original road runs parallel to the railway.

54.4 Thirsk Lake
The beginning of Thirsk Lake can be seen across the original Highway #40.

55.0 Thirsk Lake Recreation Area **Δ**
A beautiful little spot on the north shore of Thirsk Lake.

56.1 Highway #40 departs KVR.

56.3 **Milford Station** ⏐1050 🚂 ⏐ 🚲0.8
There is very little evidence of the station that once stood here.

57.6 Fills and cuts in rock.

58.6 Logging access road to Highway #40.

59.3 Kathleen Creek Bridge detour ⏐→
Take the small road to the south (left) 110 metres to the highway. Five hundred metres west on Highway #40 turn north (right) on a small road

15

Kettle Valley Railway - Princeton Subdivision
km 61.4 - km 84.3

and travel two hundred metres to reconnect with the railbed. Do not take the small road immediately after the highway bridge. This road does lead to the railway but it is on a high, loose fill.

59.6   Kathleen Creek ⨡50

The bridge over Kathleen Creek was removed by the CPR in 1995. Owing to the high, loose fills on both sides of the creek, it is best to detour using the highway bridge to cross the creek.

59.9   Kathleen Creek Bridge detour ends ⊢←

A small road from Highway #40 crosses the KVR.

61.4   Highway #40. ⊤

61.6   Access road to Highway #40. ⊤

61.9   Osprey Lake Station ⌐1095 🚂 ⛽ ⫯ 🚴0.6

The concrete water tower foundation is found 300 metres prior to the slab foundation of the station house. Just past the station the ballast has been stripped for approximately one kilometre. To the south there is a small rough airstrip running parallel to the KVR.

63.1   Osprey Lake summit ⌐1098 —private drive. ⊤

63.3   Osprey Lake)(142

A pile trestle spans the east end of Osprey Lake, across from the numerous summer cottages that line the north shore.

Before the advent of mechanical refrigeration, large amounts of ice were cut by hand from Osprey Lake during the winter months. They were transported by the KVR and stored in blocks in sawdust-insulated icehouses in Penticton. The ice was used during the summer months to cool the reefer cars transporting fruit and to supply air conditioning for railway passenger cars. Ice was also taken from Otter Lake at km 139, by the Great Northern Railway to supply their icehouses in Washington state. In 1919, 3,000 cars of ice were loaded and shipped in 15 days. By the early 1920s mechanical ice had come of age, and a rapid decline in the need for natural ice resulted.

64.4   Osprey Lake wye. Y

65.0   Link Lake Road ⊤ ⚑

A small forest service campground can be found south on Link Lake Road and another one can be found taking Link Lake Road north to Highway #40, then east to the campground.

66.0   Access road to Highway #40. ⊤

66.7   Bankeir ⫯ ⑂ 🍴 (

3 Lakes General Store is just a few metres north of the railbed. This is the only store, coffee and snack bar on the route from Penticton to Prin-

Kettle Valley Railway - Princeton Subdivision
km 84.4 - 110.4

16

ceton. Watch for Jake the border collie and yes, the horse does bite. A small road runs between the store and the right-of-way.

66.9   Highway #40. ↑

67.4   As the Hayes Creek Valley bottom falls, it leaves the KVR high on the north slope. Magnificent views of this narrow valley can be glimpsed through the trees. Ranches and swamps fill in any broadened areas of the valley.

70.5   Overlooking Chain Lake.

71.0   Chain Link Campground—access road to Highway #40 △ ↑
Located at the intersection of this road with Highway #40 is Chain Lake Campground on the shore of Chain Lake. It is 300 metres down the hill to the campground.

71.8   End of Chain Lake.

73.5   Jellicoe Station |1017 🚂 ╽ 🚲0.3
This was formerly named Usk Station but later named after the British admiral who distinguished himself at the Battle of Jutland in 1916.
   What remains of Jellicoe today is the station foundation and a root cellar in the side of the hill. There is a small red freight shed still standing less than 100 metres farther down the right-of-way. The wide railbed results from the siding that once existed here.

76.7   Access road to Highway #40. ↑

77.9   Siwash Creek
The half moon fill area that crosses Siwash Creek encircles a large cabin.

79.4   Spukunne Creek Road. ↑

80.8   Fifty Mile Tank 🏗
The water tower foundation is found slipping over the hillside.

81.0   Spukunne Creek—five through plate girder spans.)(78

85.1   Logging area near the KVR, resulting in a chewed up railbed.

85.8   Erris Station |981 🚂 ╽ 🚲0.5
Named after the mountain of the same name in Ireland. A widening in the grade and the remains of a freight shed down the side of the grade mark the location of Erris Station.

87.5   Open area and gravel pit, small trail crosses railbed.

88.1   Erris Tunnel 🚇91
Much of this 91 metre-long tunnel was excavated through loose rock, requiring wooden timbers to be used as bracing. With the timbers still

in place during the final operation of this line, it became the last timber-lined tunnel to be used on the CPR system. A metal water trough at the west exit helps keep the railbed from being washed out.

89.0   Treharne Creek

A major washout occurred here on April 9, 1934.

93.4   Scenic views down Hayes Creek Valley to Similkameen Valley.

94.6   Gate.

95.0   Mileage post 59, just prior to crossing Christian Creek.

96.2   **Sixty Mile Tank** 🛢

The octagonal foundation of the water tower remains and the right-of-way widens for the Jura siding just after the water tower.

96.6   Mileage post 60.

96.7   Jura Station ⌐930 🏠 🛢 🍴 ⅄ 🚲1.9

A siding and a wye were built at Jura where the heavy 2.2% grade eased to 1%. The wye was used for turning the helper engines. The KVR departs the Hayes Creek Valley at Jura and the railbed then crosses an open, grassy plateau speckled with small lakes and stands of pine. In spring and summer the open hills above Princeton are carpeted with wild flowers.

In 1912, a decision was made to route the KVR into Princeton. The railway, high in the Hayes Creek Valley at elevation 930 metres, had to descend 282 metres into Princeton, less than 12 kilometres away. McCulloch chose to maintain a 2.2% grade over this abrupt descent by laying out three extraordinary loops on the open rangeland northeast of Princeton.

98.1   Highway #40 ⌖

The gated fence of the Jura Stock Ranch greets you on the other side of Highway #40. Thirteen kilometres of the railbed winds its way through the ranch. Watch for cattle and city slickers on horseback looking for cattle rustlers. Don't get caught with fresh steaks in your panniers. Past the gate, the KVR begins the first of the Jura Loops as it rounds Separation Lakes and passes the Maverick Hitch 'n' Post.

100.4   Highway #40 ⌖

Gated fences prior to and after Highway #40. The entrance to Maverick Cattle Drives is just to the west.

104.3   Access road from Highway #40 to Highway #5A. ⌖

104.9   Belfort Station ⌐776 🏠 🍴 🚲1.5

This station was named after the famous French garrison in the "Jura" mountains that resisted the German invasion of 1870. The only visible evidence of Belfort Station is a noticeable widening of the right-of-way due to the past existence of a siding.

🚂 Coquihalla Agreement 🚂

Before the echoes of clanging picks and shovels subsided from the Battle of Midway, another hot spot in the war between the KVR and the VV&E started to flare up in the race to Princeton. In 1905 both railways were boasting that each would be in Princeton before the other. J.J. Hill was first out of the blocks pushing the VV&E from Midway ever closer to Princeton, while the KVR was buying up property around Princeton, not only for its own right-of-way but also to block the VV&E from entering their community. By 1907 the VV&E had reached Keremeos, and in 1909, Princeton. Passenger service out of Princeton aboard the VV&E commenced with the KVR still six months away from even starting construction at Midway. In the shadow of its competitor's success the KVR in 1910 started construction at Midway, Merritt and Penticton. In November 1911, the VV&E had tracks into Coalmont and the rich coal seams of the Tulameen Valley. Coal began flowing south in long strings of coal hoppers along with the hopes of a "coast-to-Kootenay" connection. Construction by the VV&E slowed after reaching Coalmont, confirming the fears of many that the rush to Princeton was for the coal and not to complete the line to Hope. But by the middle of 1912, with the sound of KVR steam engines breathing over the VV&E's shoulder, the fight to claim the narrow Coquihalla Valley commenced. The difficulty was that, owing to the extreme ruggedness of the valley, it was not practical to construct two independent railways through this constricted gouge. The surveys by the two railways through the canyon placed each with the upper hand in different sections. It became clearly evident that the duplication of what would be the most expensive section of railway in North America was unjustified.

The two competitors came together in the spring of 1913 and agreed to work on a single line, thereby bridging the final piece of the coast-to-Kootenay dream. This became known as the Coquihalla Agreement. As per the terms of that agreement, the VV&E completed the trackage from Princeton to Brookmere and granted running rights to the KVR. In exchange, the KVR agreed to build and maintain the line from Brookmere to Hope and grant running rights to the VV&E for the annual fee of 2.5% of the total cost of construction. With this agreement the VV&E and the KVR both realized the dream of the coast-to-Kootenay rail link.

106.0   Highway #40 �🇹
The KVR is earth bermed to restrict motorized vehicle traffic.

108.9   Private drive. �🇹

109.1   Allison Creek
Loose sharp rocks make up the railbed.

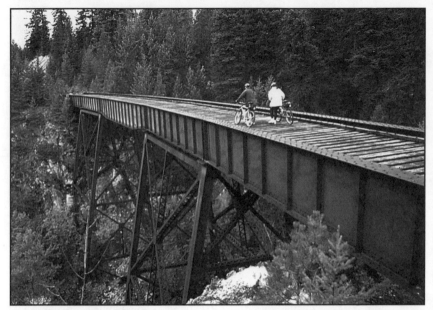

Crossing Spukunne Creek bridge, km 81.0.

Upon leaving Princeton you pass through this 324 metre-long tunnel at km 114.8. The railway then leads to a popular spot beside the Tulameen River.

Princeton

NOT TO SCALE

109.4 Rainbow Lake Road ⳤ Ⅹ 🛈 🍴 🏃

Following the road to the east brings you to the old stone ruins of the Portland Cement Plant finished in 1908. It took four years to build and yet was in operation for only nine months due to a lack of coal and limestone. This building was a grand architectural and engineering achievement of the times. The VV&E also constructed a spur from the line across the Similkameen River up Allison Creek to the plant in 1908. This line continued 700 metres past the plant, weaving its way up the creek, and crossing it five times to reach the tramway that came down from the mine.

The Portland Cement Plant is now the site of the Princeton Castle Resort. This resort covers 110 acres and has many services, such as a campsite, restaurant, hiking trails and tours of the historic ruins.

109.9 Overlooking Princeton Castle RV Park.

111.4 Old Hedley Road and Sawmill spur ⳤ ⳤ

KVR is high on the hillside overlooking the Princeton Sawmill. The spur line follows down the hill to the sawmill.

112.4 Tulameen River ⳤ*67*

A highway bridge running parallel to the west can be used to cross the river.

Kettle Valley Railway - Princeton Subdivision
km 110.4 - km 134.8

112.8   Highway #3

Just before you cross Highway #3 you find that a car dealership is using the right-of-way as a parking lot.

113.3   Vermilion Avenue. ⊤

113.4   Princeton Station i648 🚋 ⛽ ⬤ Y ⛺ ⛩ ⬤ ‖ ⬤ ⼕ (🅿️0.4

Prior to 1860 Princeton was known as Vermilion Forks, "Vermilion" meaning the mercuric sulphide compound that produces a brilliant red pigment, and "Forks" because the Similkameen and Tulameen rivers converge here. In 1860, Vermilion Forks was renamed Princeton, after the Prince of Wales.

The mercuric sulphide compound is found in the red earth up the Tulameen River. Tulameen is a Salish Indian word meaning red earth. The Indians commonly used this pigment for face painting. This feature was so prized by the Indians that many tribes would come to trade for it.

🚂 Princeton Museum 🚂
117 Vermilion Avenue, 295-7588

The abandoned Princeton Station is still standing, white vinyl sided and home to a real estate office and a Subway restaurant. Just past the station site is the junction of the Copper Mountain Subdivision. West of Princeton, the KVR trains operated on the VV&E tracks as far as Brookmere. At Brookmere the VV&E then joined onto the KVR line. The KVR's use of the track was permitted under the "Tulameen Agreement" of 1914. Only a few VV&E trains even ran as far west as Coalmont, and ultimately the trackage was sold to CPR in 1945.

114.0   Auburn Crescent. ⊤

114.2   Copper Mountain Subdivision. ⱽ (see page 138)

114.8   Tunnel ⬛324

This 324 metre-long tunnel was constructed in 1910 by the VV&E and carries the railway under Highway #3.

115.3   Tulameen River)(96

In 1885 the Tulameen River and its tributaries were the site of a gold rush. Placer gold and platinum were mined from Princeton up to Champion Creek. Present-day prospectors still search for their fortunes along the watershed of the Tulameen.

115.5   Tulameen Coal Mines spur ⱽ

A short spur ran downstream along the side of the river.

116.2   Washout

A single track against the red cliffs bypasses the washout.

18

N

Thynne Lake

153.3

152.7
152.5
152.1
151.7

151.0

Manning Creek

149.8
149.6
149.1

Manning

ASPEN GROVE STAGE ROAD

Otter Creek

147.5

Frembd Lake

Elliot Creek

146.8

Frembd Creek

146.1

MOUNT SPEARING

BOULDER MOUNTAIN

Perley Cr

144.2

Lockie Cr

Riddell Cr

142.4

Otter Lake

MOUNT RIDDELL

Kettle Valley Railway - Princeton Subdivision
km 134.8 - 154.4

| 0 | 1 | 2 | 3 | 4 km |

| 0 | 1 | 2 | 3 miles |

Tulameen

OTTER MOUNTAIN

139.2

138.8
138.1

Cook Cr

137.6

Tulameen River

137.0

Collins Gulch

136.0

116.3   Pleasant Valley Mining spur Ɏ
        Another short spur crossed the river to a tipple.

116.6   The Tulameen River shows the reason for its name with bright red banks
        framing a blue river.

117.7   Washout
        Does not affect cyclists.

118.0   Hoodoos.

119.0   Coalmont Road is suspended high on the slope above the KVR. The
        walls of the canyon are unstable resulting in a constant flow of rubble
        cascading down on the KVR. Over the next few kilometres prepare to
        do a lot of rock dodging.

121.0   Parr Ɏ

        The name Parr came from the name of the engineer in charge of the tunnel
        construction. Parr was the name of the short spur at this location. Origi-
        nally two bridges took 1.5 kilometres of the railway along the south bank
        of the Tulameen River. On January 25, 1935, an ice jam washed out one of
        the bridges on which the railway crossed. Repairs were not completed
        until February 11, 1935. Continuing difficulties in maintaining the two
        bridges resulted in the construction of the tunnel. The tunnel was built in
        1948-49, allowing 1.3 kilometres of the railway to relocate to the north
        bank of the river, bypassing the two bridges. The railbed, with rotting ties
        still in place, can be seen across the river and the remains of the abutments
        of the two bridges against the banks of the river.

        Roaneys, a former flagstop, was located on the bypassed section at
        km 121.5.

122.0   Parr Tunnel ◖147
        Owing to the curvature of this 147 metre-long tunnel, both ends of the
        tunnel cannot be seen when in the middle.

122.5   Slight washout on left side of railbed, does not affect cycling.

123.0   Major washout
        One hundred and fifty metres of railbed is washout right down to the
        riverbed. At normal river levels the riverbed can be crossed. Some dif-
        ficulty may be encountered getting down and up the steep loose rock
        sides of the railbed.

125.0   Washout, railbed down to single track for 70 metres.

125.2   Tulameen River)(71
        Through truss bridge with small red shack on the north end.

125.4   Roany Creek—minor washout.

125.9   Minor washout.

126.7   Major washout
The railbed is washout down to the riverbed for 190 metres. Again the riverbed can be crossed, the only difficulty is getting down and up the sides of the railgrade.

127.0   Beautiful rust-coloured slope falling down to the river. Coalmont Road hangs precariously high above on the wall of the canyon.

127.3   Washout
Railbed missing for 80 metres with a single track along the edge.

128.2   Washout
The railbed is down to a single track for a short distance.

128.4   Tulameen River)(105
Rust-coloured cliffs provide a contrasting backdrop to the green pines and blue waters of the Tulameen River. The end of the washouts and a well-packed railbed make for a pleasant cycle to Coalmont. The sandy beach on the west end of the bridge invites you to take a dip.

130.7   Granite Creek
Across the Tulameen River was the site of Granite City, named after Granite Creek, which enters the Tulameen River at this point. Granite City became a bustling town of about 2,000 after the discovery of these gold-laden waters in 1885. In 1886 Granite City was considered the largest city in the interior of British Columbia. However, when the gold boom ended less than four years later, the town became deserted. The mounds of tailings and a few dilapidated log buildings lost amongst the trees are all that remain.

One of the frustrations of panning the placer gold on Granite Creek was a white metal of similar weight intermixed with the gold. Hence, it was difficult to separate the two. Years later it was discovered that the white metal was platinum, with a value well exceeding that of the gold. There was a renewed interest in Granite Creek as prospectors reworked old claims and searched for the discarded piles of platinum.

132.1   Coalmont-Tulameen Road Ϯ Λ ⚑ ▮ ⫽ ☙ (
The Coalmont Hotel still operates among the false-fronted wooden buildings on Main Street. It was recently restored with original antique decor including the sleeping units, a public dining area and pub. Also found in Coalmont is the Coalmont General Store just north of the hotel. To reach Granite Creek Forestry Campground, 1.6 kilometres from the hotel, follow Bettes Avenue through Coalmont and across the Tulameen River, turn left on Blakeburn Road, then left on Rice Road. This leads you to the campground and the site of Granite City. The remains of Blakeburn can be found about five kilometres up Blakeburn Road.

132.3 Coalmont Station ¡727 🚂 ⫿ ⫿ ⫿ 🔔0.6

Named for the seemingly endless "mountain of coal" in the area. Now almost a ghost town, Coalmont flourished in the early 1900s when J. J. Hill's VV&E reached Coalmont and immediately started transporting coal from the Columbia Coal and Coke Company to the iron horses of the Great Northern Railway. The surface coal was quickly spent and it soon proved uneconomical to mine the deeper coal seams. As mines in the area disappeared, so did the residents of Coalmont.

133.0 Coalmont—Tulameen Road. ⫿

136.0 Gated fence for cow pasture.

137.0 Gated fence ends cow pasture.

137.6 Coalmont—Tulameen Road. ⫿

138.1 Otter Creek.)(13

138.6 2nd Street—Tulameen. 🏛 ⫿ ⫿ ⫿

Coalmont General Store, km 132.1.

138.8 Tulameen Station ¡763 🚂 ⫿ ⫿ ⫿ 🔔0.2

This area was called Campement des Femmes, "Camp of the Women." When the men went into the countryside to hunt, Salish Indian women and children were left here on this fertile flat, which served as a base camp. During the Gold Rush, the area was known as Otter Flats and later renamed Tulameen.

Had there not been the threat of the KVR beating J. J. Hill's VV&E to the coast, Hill would have preferred to construct a grade west from here up the Tulameen River Valley. Approximately at the intersection of Railway Creek and the Tulameen River, an eight mile-long tunnel was to be constructed through the Hope Mountains to emerge at Dewdney Creek in the Coquihalla River Valley. Such a tunnel would have taken years to construct. The restraint of time played a part in the final route chosen, as the KVR and VV&E raced to the Coquihalla River Valley since it was wide enough for only one rail line.

A spur ran from here to the shore of Otter Lake Provincial Park beach where the VV&E cut ice from the lake to feed its ice houses in Washington state. Each year thousands of boxcars of ice made their way south.

The Tulameen Station built in 1914 was moved within the townsite and now serves as a private residence. An old red freight shed has been moved a short distance from the railbed and can be seen in use as a storage shed.

139.2 Otter Lake)(102 ⫿

Just before you cross the outlet of Otter Lake you come to Otter Lake Provincial Park. A second section of the park is found 4.6 kilometres north on the west side of the lake. The southern parcel of the park has picnicking and swimming, and the northern parcel has camping and swimming. The KVR follows the east side of Otter Lake constrained between the shore and the steep mountainsides.

142.4   A beautiful little campsite on the lakeshore in a small rock cut beside the railway. 🏕

144.2   Gate.

146.1   Otter Creek)(37

Just downstream of the confluence of Otter Creek and Frembd Creek, the KVR crosses Otter Creek to travel the west side of the valley.

146.8   Frembd Lake

The KVR squeezes along the narrow valley between the steep forested mountain slopes and Frembd Lake.

147.5   Otter Creek)(14

A pile trestle crosses an old channel of Otter Creek.

149.1   Otter Creek)(41

The KVR again crosses back to the east side of the valley.

149.4   Pasture

The railway grade has been removed by a local rancher for the next 400 metres.

149.6   Manning Station |785 🚂 ⬢🚲0.5

With the exception of a widening of the right-of-way and some scattered concrete pieces, there is not much evidence of Manning Station. Local ranchers in the area have placed fences up across the KVR. Some of the fences may be difficult to open. Past Manning the KVR continues to cross and recross the serpentine Otter Creek.

149.8   Manning Creek)(9 ☨

Double pile trestles, one for the main line and one for the siding, cross the creek. The railbed resumes and crosses a small road.

150.5   Washouts

A number of small washouts in the next 200 metres.

151.0   Otter Creek)(27

The end of the trestle is partially washed out.

151.7   Otter Creek.)(27

152.1   Otter Creek.)(41

152.5   Otter Creek)(27

The washed-out south abutment of this trestle was bridged by a great bunch of cyclists dedicated to the preservation of the railway as a trail.

152.6 Washed-out gully through railbed.

152.7 Otter Creek.)(32

153.3 Thynne Lake
With the lake pressed against the valley's east wall, the KVR skirts the west shore of Thynne Lake.

155.5 Gate.

156.8 Otter Creek.)(27

157.5 Private drive
A log fence lines a private drive requiring a hop over the two fences or a walk around the front of the entrance.

157.8 Otter Creek.)(37

160.2 Private drive. ⍭

161.1 Gate.

162.2 Rockfall.

164.6 Gate.

164.7 Youngsberg Road ⍭ ⊢⇒
Gravel barricade just south of the road. The trestle over Otter Creek and Aspen Grove Stage Road was burned down. To avoid climbing down the steep fill and boulder hopping across Otter Creek, detour west (left) on Youngsberg Road (130 metres). Turn north (right) on Aspen Grove Stage Road and cross the bridge and cattle guard (820 metres), then turn west (left) on to the small road just in front of the gravel abutment of the missing trestle. Follow the road up to the railbed (340 metres).
    Following Youngsberg Road east there are primitive forestry service campsites at the fishing lakes of Thalia, Goose and Lodwick.

165.2 Aspen Grove Stage Road and Otter Creek ✠61
This frame and pile trestle was set ablaze in 1996. It is possible to climb down the steep gravel abutments and boulder hop across Otter Creek with some difficulty.
    Just north of the east abutment is a cave used by the famous CPR train robber, Bill Miner. The KVR did not exist when Bill Miner was robbing trains.

165.6 Detour road joins railbed. ⊢⇐

Kettle Valley Railway - Princeton Subdivision
km 153.1 - km 174.4

19

165.7 Thalia Station |866 🚂 ⫰ 🚴1.9

This station was formerly named Canyon.

167.4 Major washout

The local residents have built a 110 metre-long bypass road alongside the washed-out railbed.

167.7 Canyon narrows

The railbed and the creek fit shoulder to shoulder through this tight canyon.

168.5 Spearing Station |917 🚂 ⫰ Δ🚴0.9

This was formerly named Koyl Station, but the name was changed when confusion was noted between it and Coyle Station on the Merritt Sub-division. Spearing was named after Gus Spearing, a civil war veteran who spent his final days trapping in the Otter Valley.

Today you will find Burt's Horse Motel, a privately owned camp-ground for horse owners. Cyclists are welcome.

172.3 Spearing Creek.)(27

173.6 Brookmere Road ⸸ Δ

A rough campsite used mainly in the winter by snowmobiles.

174.1 Gate.

174.5 Brookmere community grounds.

174.8 Private drive. ⸸

174.9 Brookmere Station |962 🚂 ⫰ ⫰ ⫰

This area was originally known as Otter Summit, and later named Brook-mere with the coming of the railway. Brookmere was the divisional point of the KVR from the VV&E tracks. The presence of the two railways ac-counted for an unusual nature to the Brookmere railway yard. The KVR and GNR shared the station house and locomotive watering facilities. This created the unique feature of having Brookmere Station squarely in the middle of the yard so that it would equally serve both railways. Similarly, the water tank at the west end of the yard was equipped with a spout on each side to permit use by either railway. North of the tracks, the KVR built a bunkhouse, coal tower, turntable and a three-stall roundhouse.

You will find that many of the KVR buildings have been preserved at Brookmere. The water tower was relocated for preservation, and a wooden caboose was also given as a gift from the town of Merritt to the citizens of Brookmere. Brookmere is one of the few towns on this route that has been able to preserve some of its railroad heritage.

The Brookmere Station House is now a private museum owned and operated by Harry Fontaine. It should not be missed. Call ahead to make sure Harry will be there: (250) 378-9645.

COALMONT
ROAD

Princeton
0.0
3.4
0.7
1.4
5.3
5.8

N

COPPER MOUNTAIN ROAD

Bromley Creek

9.6
Allenby

11.5

Similkameen

Wolfe Creek

15.4

16.6
Smelter Lakes

River

CM

Copper Mountain
21.4

22.4

Kettle Valley Railway - Copper Mountain Subdivision
km 0.0 - km 21.4

0   1   2   3   4 km

0   1   2   3 miles

COPPER MOUNTAIN SUBDIVISION
Princeton to Copper Mountain, 21.4 kilometres

In the early 1900s, Canada Copper owned a mine on Copper Mountain, just south of Princeton. With an increased demand for copper during the First World War, Canada Copper approached the KVR in April of 1917 requesting that a rail line be constructed from Princeton to Copper Mountain. The KVR would haul raw ore from Copper Mountain Mine to a concentrator plant that was to be built between the mine and Princeton, then to the smelter at Trail, B.C. By November 1917, McCulloch had completed the survey work and by the spring of the next year, construction began.

With the work involved and wartime shortages, this branch line was not completed until October 1920. The Copper Mountain Subdivision ran for 21.4 kilometres, and included 24 trestles and four tunnels. One section even required 360,000 cubic yards of solid rock to be blasted from the mountainside to create a ledge for the track. A secondary spur ran to the top of the concentrator mill, a site called Allenby. Both Copper Mountain and Allenby had turntables in order to turn locomotives around for the return trip.

After only a few months of operation, depressed postwar copper prices closed the mine in December 1920. Canada Copper then sold the mine to Granby Consolidated Mining and Smelting Company. Granby reopened the mine in August 1925, for an extremely productive period of five years. During this time, the KVR had a 15-car ore train making three round trips per day between the mine and mill. In an average year, the KVR handled 13,696 cars of ore and 861 cars of concentrates along this line.

Late in 1930, the mine closed only to again reopen in 1937. Copper prices had increased due to the Spanish Civil War, along with an increased demand for copper when Canada entered the Second World War. The Copper Mountain Mine and rail line operated continuously for the next 20 years, but in April of 1957 the mine again closed, this time permanently. Shortly afterwards, the Copper Mountain Subdivision was abandoned and the line dismantled.

Today, the original railbed is in rideable condition from Princeton to km 16.5. Unfortunately, the route is discontinuous because of the missing bridge across the Similkameen River and the construction of houses on the right-of-way. Pieces of this subdivision are slowly being sold off. On the loops overlooking Princeton, a residential development already has the right-of-way running into someone's outdoor swimming pool at km 3.4. Farther along, at km 5.8 the front door of Tanglewood Hollow abruptly stops further progress. If there was a way to get around the private property, you would find the railbed to Allenby is in good condition. Of course, it is possible to cycle from Allenby to the back of the property.

For the determined mountain biker who needs to do it all, it is possible to access all the discontinuous sections between those privately held. The flat and dusty 6.1 kilometre-long section reclaimed by Allenby Road, from Allenby to the locked gate into Copper Mountain just short of

Smelter Lakes, can also be tackled. Past Smelter Lakes, the forest and time have reclaimed this most fascinating section of the KVR with all its trestles and tunnels, making it totally impassable. The remains of the trestles and the abandoned tunnels still clinging to the side of the Similkameen Canyon on this impassable section can be viewed from the Newmont Mines just across the canyon ▄▄

Using 24 trestles and four tunnels, this 21.4 kilometre-long branch line ascended nearly 300 metres from Princeton to the mine on Copper Mountain. (Princeton Museum)

km **Princeton Station** i*648* 🚂 🏠 ⫝ ⫞→
0.0
A detour is necessary because of the missing bridge over the Similkameen River and the rough shape of the KVR from Princeton to Allenby. From the boarded up Princeton Station head east on Highway #3 and hang a right (north) on to Copper Mountain Road. After a muscle tiring climb of 5.3 kilometres, turn east (right) on to Allenby Road. 2.9 kilometres down Allenby Road is the remains of the Allenby concentrator mill. At this site, Allenby Road turns on to the original KVR grade.

0.7   Copper Mountain Subdivision departs from Princeton Subdivision. ⫝

1.4   Similkameen River. ⋈*122*

3.4   Private residence
The right-of-way runs into the outdoor pool of the private residence.

3.5   Access road to Copper Mountain Road. ⫞⇐

5.3   East Similkameen Road. ⫞⇒ ⫞⇐

5.8   Tanglewood Hollow
The KVR runs right into the front door of this private residence. It is difficult to bypass without trespassing.

9.6   **Allenby** 🚂 🏠 ⫝ ⨯ ⫞←
The decaying remains of the old concentrator mill are found in every direction. The majority of it is hiding in the vegetation surrounding the main site. Up the hill, behind where the plant stood, is the High Line spur, which the KVR used to deliver the raw ore to the concentrator. From Allenby to Smelter Lakes, Allenby Road runs on top of the original railbed with a few jogs to bypass missing trestles.

11.5   High Line spur ⫝
This 2.6 kilometre-long spur heads back to the top of the old concentrator plant at Allenby. This spur line is marginally passable, being rather rough and overgrown.

15.4   Locked gate into Copper Mountain.

16.6   Smelter Lakes ⋈*233*
Smelter Lakes no longer exist in reality. Years of dumping tailings into the lakes have completely filled the narrow valley. At this point the road leaves the railway grade and climbs the valley wall along Smelter Lakes. The KVR is not passable beyond this point, even on foot, as the forest has reclaimed the grade and the tunnel portals are blocked by slides. In this last 5.8 kilometres the railway had 17 trestles and four tunnels. Many of the trestles still cling to the side of the Similkameen Valley.

21.4 **Copper Mountain.** 🚂 ⫝

22.4   Turntable and end of line.

Kettle Valley Railway
Merritt Subdivision
Brookmere to Merritt
47.3 km

Kettle Valley Railway – Merritt Subdivision Profile

MERRITT SUBDIVISION
Brookmere to Merritt, 47.3 kilometres

The section of the Kettle Valley Railway between Brookmere and Merritt is known as the Merritt Subdivision. This subdivision was not part of the KVR coast-to-Kootenay main line, but was simply a branch line to connect the KVR main line with the CPR main line. However, this branch line was frequently used during the winter season when the Coquihalla Subdivision was closed because of heavy snow or damages, forcing trains to be diverted north. After the permanent closure of the Coquihalla Subdivision in 1959, the Merritt Subdivision became part of the KVR main line.

The pleasant cycle through this short section is very scenic as you follow the Coldwater River Valley on a gentle downhill grade and well-travelled railbed. This route passes through the Coldwater River Canyon with high rock walls to either side as both the railbed and the river squeeze through the canyon along the valley bottom. The valley then opens up to rolling hills covered with grass and speckled with pine trees as it leads you into the city of Merritt nestled in the Nicola Valley.

The only designated campsites or lodging facilities along the Merritt Subdivision are in Merritt. So if you have stayed at Coalmont (89 kilometres from Merritt) or at Otter Lake (82 kilometres from Merritt), you have a bit of an endurance challenge in store to push and pedal the distance. You may have to set up a backcountry campsite along the railbed. Many backcountry camping opportunities exist around Brodie. However, your legs will be pleased that the trail is a good one and the grade falls gently downhill from Brookmere. Once you've made it to Merritt, you can easily reward yourself as all amenities are available to you in this friendly town in the Nicola Valley ▬

km	**Brookmere Station** |1962 🚋 🏠)
0.0	Brookmere was a busy railway town in its day, being the junction point for the three subdivisions of the Kettle Valley Railway, Princeton, Coquihalla and Merritt. It was also the junction point of the VV&E line. Brookmere is presently a quiet little community with a few KVR buildings and a wooden caboose and water tower preserved in memory of Brookmere's KVR history.
0.4	Brookmere Road. k
1.1	Brook Creek.)(
1.3	Brook Creek.)(
2.8	Brook Creek.)(
	Railbed is composed of large, loose gravel and is a little better packed where the tire tracks are.

20

Kettle Valley Railway - Merritt Subdivision
km 0.0 - km 25.9

5.4 Major washout

Thirty metres of railbed has been swept off the face of the mountain. A trail cuts up and through the trees and around the missing railbed.

5.9 Sand slide

Fifty metres of the railbed is covered by a sand slide.

6.4 **Brodie** ᵢ923 🚃 ⸮ ⸎ 𝔸ᴮ 🚲₀.₉.

This spot on the KVR was known as "the Loop." Brodie Station was at the apex of this large loop, where the main line turned back on itself to continue north along the branch line to Merritt. At this apex, the main line continued south on the Coquihalla Subdivision to Hope.

Brodie can be accessed from Coquihalla Highway by the Larson Hill exit (Exit 250) and taking Brodie Siding Road following down along the highway.

All around Brodie is some of the most beautiful backcountry camping spots on the KVR. The only drawback is the highway noise from the Coquihailla.

6.6 Coldwater River—through-plate girder)(3₁

This is one of the more beautiful sections of the KVR with the railway and the Coldwater River continually trading sides as each tries to gain the advantage through the narrow Coldwater River Canyon. Because of the tight quarters with the walls of the canyon, there are frequent rockfalls requiring a lot of rock dodging along this section.

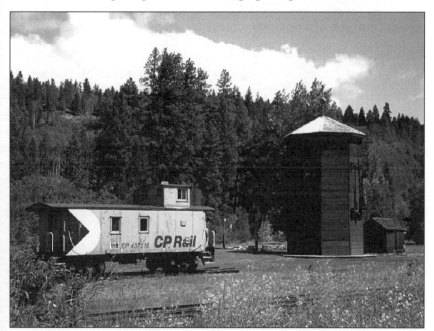

An original CPR wooden caboose and KVR water tower are found at Brookmere, km 0.0.

Railbed washed away along shore of Coldwater River, km 25.9.

Railbed is completely washed away approaching this through truss over the Coldwater River, km 40.4.

7.4   Coldwater River—pony truss.)(33

7.6   Coldwater River—deck truss.)(33

8.4   Coldwater River—deck truss.)(33

8.6   Coldwater River—deck truss.)(33

12.1   Coldwater River—through truss.)(34

12.4   Gate—Coldwater Road. ⋆

16.0   Coquihalla Highway Overpass/access to KVR ⋆
        Coldwater Road, KVR and the Coldwater River pass under the Coqui-
        halla Highway. Access to both Coldwater Road and Coquihalla High-
        way can be gained here. Exit 256 from the Coquihalla Highway will
        bring you to this place.

16.9   Minor washout.

18.6   Kingsvale Station |817 🚂 🏕 ⅃ 🚴0.8
        The station house still stands in this picturesque little community and
        is presently occupied as a private residence. Between the station house
        and the bridge is the concrete foundation of the water tower. Past
        Kingsvale the KVR enters farmland and with it comes the problem of
        gates and fences.

18.7   Coldwater Road / Voght Creek.)(20

23.0   Gate.

23.2   Peterson Road. ⋆

24.6   Peterson Road ⋆ ⊦⇨
        There are two reasons to detour at this point. One, the railbed is washed
        out at km 25.9 and nearly impossible to cross and two, the Coldwater
        Indian Reserve does not allow cyclists on the railbed through the re-
        serve. Detour by taking Peterson Road up to Coldwater Road. Go north
        on Coldwater Road to a small unmarked road that leads down to the
        Merritt Mountain Music Festival grounds.

24.8   Olsons spur. ⌐

25.0   Road ⋆
        A small road leads down to the river or up to Peterson Road.

25.9   Major washout
        One hundred and eighty metres of railbed was washed away when the
        Coldwater River changed its course. This is a very difficult washout to

21

Kettle Valley Railway - Merritt Subdivision
km 25.4 - km 47.3

Merritt

get through with a bike. High water levels may make it impossible. If so, detour on Peterson Road.

26.6   Sand slide.

27.5   Sand slide.

28.1   Private drive

The KVR becomes marginally passable for a few hundred metres before Pine, due to rubble and a disruption of the railbed. You can detour this disruption by taking Patchet Road, which parallels the northeast side of the railbed. After a couple of hundred metres, this road crosses the KVR to then intersect with the Coldwater Road. You can reaccess the KVR at this crossing. Past this point, the right-of-way passes though a farmyard that has gated fences at both ends.

28.3   Patchet Road ⌁ |→

Last exit before Coldwater Indian Reserve.

28.4   Pine |764 |/ 🚲0.9

A 24.1 kilometre-long logging spur was constructed here in the 1920s by the Nicola Pine Mill of Merritt. Operated by the mill, the line was extended along Midday Creek as logging operations proceeded up the valley. Operation of the spur line ended in the Depression years of the 1930s.

32.2   Glenwalker Station |697 🚃 🚲0.7

This section is again in the midst of farm land. When passing through this stretch, you may find irrigation sprinklers on, watering not only the crops, but also the railbed and you. This can actually be quite nice, especially if you are cycling in the heat of the day. There is a private road from the station to Coldwater Road.

32.6   Entering Coldwater Indian Reserve

A gravel barricade and ditch erected to inhibit traffic through the reserve marks the Coldwater Indian Reserve boundary. When the right-of-way of the Kettle Valley Railway was acquired by the government of British Columbia, the railbed that was contained within the boundaries of the Indian reserves were turned over to the respective reserves. The Coldwater Indian Reserve has denied any request to cycle the railbed through their property.

36.1   Access road to Coldwater Road ⌁

This access road crosses the railbed, then continues across the Coldwater River. There is a small residential community to the west.

39.2   Exiting Coldwater Indian Reserve

A gravel barricade across the right-of-way blocks vehicle traffic.

40.4 Coldwater River—through truss)(34

The Coldwater River has cut a new channel that has removed the railbed south of the bridge. The bridge now sits on its naked south abutment in the middle of the river. The river can be forded only at low water levels.

42.3 Coldwater River—through truss)(34

The northern approach has been washed out and the north abutment has been undermined, twisting the through-truss bridge. The river can be forded only at low water levels.

43.1 Access road—Merritt Mountain Music Festival grounds ↑ ⊣←

The only access road to the KVR after the Coldwater Indian Reserve.

The Merritt Mountain Music Festival is a weekend-long music festival held in July. From here to Pooley Avenue the KVR is used as a road from the festival grounds to Merritt.

45.2 Access road from Pooley Avenue ↑ ⊢⇒

Past this point the KVR is under constant change and may not be passable.

45.8 Douglas Street ↑ ⊢→

Weyerhauser Sawmill yard has swallowed up the railbed of the KVR.

46.3 Merritt Mine spur

This 1.4 kilometre-long spur was built in 1907 to reach the Middlesboro Collieries across the Coldwater River.

47.3 Merritt Station |567 ▬ ⬛ ♪ |/ Υ Δ ♨ �🌲 ⬛ (

Merritt was originally a flag stop along the Nicola Branch Line of the CPR. This CPR branch line was formally opened in April 1907 as the Nicola, Kamloops & Similkameen Railway, later changed to the CPR's Nicola Branch Line. It ran between Spences Bridge and Nicola giving CPR access to the wealth of coal in the Nicola Valley for their locomotives.

It was here at Merritt that the Kettle Valley Railway connected to the CPR's Nicola Branch Line. The KVR opened the Merritt Subdivision May 1915. It was October 1915, that the Nicola Branch Line was turned over to the Kettle Valley Railway, enabling the KVR trains to run directly through to Spences Bridge, the junction point of the CPR main line.

Merritt

NOT TO SCALE

▰▰▱▱ **Nicola Valley Museum Archives** ▱▱▰▰
(2202 Jackson, 378-4145)

The tracks along the Merritt Subdivision were some of the last to be removed from the Kettle Valley Railway. The abandoned Merritt Station has been moved and can still be found along the NK&S east of Merritt. Merritt became a growing centre with the coming of the railway. Cattle and mining are still an important part of Merritt's economy. With the Coquihalla Highway passing through Merritt, just as the KVR did so many years earlier, this city is again a hub of activity.

Kettle Valley Railway
Coquihalla Subdivision
Brookmere to Hope
91.1 km

Kettle Valley Railway – Coquihalla Subdivision Profile

IMPORTANT NOTICE

A significant portion of the railbed in the Coquihalla Subdivision is owned by Trans Mountain Pipeline Company. This portion of the railway is not open to public access. The Trans Canada Trail Foundation is presently (summer 1998) in the process of trying to come to an agreement with Trans Mountain Pipeline Company for the use of the railbed and the Trans Mountain Pipeline Road as part of the Trans Canada Trail. Until such an agreement is reached, anyone who enters on to this railbed without Trans Mountain Pipline's permission is trespassing. Check the website http://www.planet.eon.net/~dan/ for updates on this situation.

COQUIHALLA SUBDIVISION
Brookmere to Hope, 91.1 kilometres

The final section of the Kettle Valley Railway, the Coquihalla Subdivision, was constructed in July 1916, completing the coast-to-Kootenay connection. The country through the Coquihalla Valley is magnificent and rugged, with high mountains and sheer rock cliffs reaching into the canyon below. It is ironic that Andrew McCulloch named the Coquihalla stations after characters from the plays of Shakespeare, in seemingly vast contrast to the rugged countryside around him. The rail line along this route is nothing more than a narrow ledge tucked up on the side of a steep canyon, with huge bridges and impressive timber trestles. It is no wonder that many stories were generated by the fact that the passenger train happened to travel this section at night thus preventing the passengers from seeing the rocky cliff edges and the canyon far below.

The path carved through the Coquihalla by the Kettle Valley Railway fell silent the winter of 1959, and was shortly thereafter abandoned. However, the Coquihalla again saw activity in 1985 with the construction of the Coquihalla Highway. Following basically the same path as the KVR, the highway consequently faced many similar obstacles such as dealing with both the ungiving terrain and weather of the Cascade Mountains and with the overly high construction and maintenance costs. A toll booth is operational on the Coquihalla Highway to help cover some of these costs.

Cycling the 91.1 kilometres of the Coquihalla Subdivision from Brookmere to Hope lets you experience the sheer magnificence and harshness of this backcountry. The ride is not entirely easy going, because you are often off the less challenging grade of the railbed. Only half of the total distance cycled is actually upon the railbed itself. The reason for this is that many of the trestles are no longer safe for travel or even standing, some tunnels are collapsed, and at some spots the grade itself has been wiped off the side of the cliff. The main detour routes used are the Transmountain Pipeline Road and the Coquihalla Highway, both of which follow very closely or atop the original KVR grade.

You begin pedaling this section from the town of Brookmere along the easy downhill grade toward Brodie. Past Brodie, you begin your ascent to the summit at Coquihalla Station. Impressive views await you all along this none-too-scenic route. Past Coquihalla Summit, keep cranking along the Transmountain Pipeline Road for the next 23 kilometres. The grade of this road is as expected—variable. At times you are atop the railway grade, and at other times you are viewing the railway's haggard remains clinging to the cliffs above. At km 54.5 the pipeline road turns to join the Coquihalla Highway.

The asphalt of the highway now becomes your travel route for the next 20 kilometres. Get ready for one long downhill boogie, and some attractive mountain scenes. You leave the highway to rejoin the railbed at Othello and the Quintette Tunnels. This is a truly spectacular spot where the thun-

22

N

Brodie

6.6
6.9
6.4

5

13.1

13.9

Juliet 15.5
15.8
16.2
16.4

Kettle Valley Railway - Coquihalla Subdivision
km 6.4 - km 26.2

0   1   2   3   4 km

0   1   2   3 miles

Juliet   Creek

18.2

MOUNT THYNNE

22.2

22.8
23.1

Coldwater

5

26.4   26.2
26.6

dering Coquihalla River carves its way through a sheer rock canyon. The railway hangs on the cliff wall, passing through tunnels and crossing over bridges in order to share this narrow canyon with the raging Coquihalla River below. Once through the last tunnel, a great cruiser ride awaits you. The railbed is packed gravel lined with a lush growth of coastal vegetation, encouraged by the high rainfall of this area. The railbed leads you to Kawkawa Lake Road, which in turn leads into Hope.

The time needed to cycle this section is one to two days, depending on your ability and endurance level. Since the only designated camping facilities are at Othello or in Hope, you may have to set up a backcountry campsite along route. We strongly recommend taking time to cycle the Coquihalla, a place where two things take your breath away—the excellent scenery and the challenging ride ⛟

km	
	Brookmere Station ⏐*1962* 🚂 👤 ⁾ 🚴*0.6*
0.0	Brookmere Station was the divisional point between the KVR line and the VV&E line. The Coquihalla Agreement of 1913 allowed GNR to use the KVR tracks from Brookmere to Hope for a payment of $150,000 per year. It was felt by some that this healthy payment was all that kept the CPR from abandoning the line in the 1930s. In 1944, GNR had to pay $4.5 million to cancel the agreement after only one GNR train had used the line in September of 1916. This was no doubt the most expensive train ride in the history of railroads. The railbed is easily cycled for the next 18 kilometres, from Brookmere to Juliet except for two washouts at kms 13.1 and 13.9.

6.4   Brodie Station ⏐*1923* 🚂 ⁾ 🚴*0.9*
Apex of "the loop," where the railway tracks branch, the Merritt Subdivision going north and the Coquihalla Subdivision going south. The Coquihalla Highway can be accessed from Brodie by following the 4x4 road that runs alongside the highway heading north to the Larson Hill Exit (Exit 250).

6.6   Coldwater River—deck truss Δ^6 ⱨ*33*
The bridge cannot be crossed. The west abutment has been undermined by the Coldwater River causing the bridge to twist. Take the Merritt Subdivision bridge across the Coldwater River, then backtrack the few metres to the Coquihalla Subdivision railbed.

6.9   Coquihalla Highway—Brodie Siding Road ⱦ
Just before the KVR intersects the Coquihalla Highway it crosses Brodie Siding Road. The railbed is lost due to the construction of the highway over it but by detouring on Brodie Siding Road to the south and crossing under the bridge of the highway, the KVR can again be picked up. On the west side of the highway the railbed is utilized by Brodie Siding Road all the way to Juliet.

The first of two major washouts just north of Juliet, km 13.1.

Bridalveil Falls, km 34.1.

13.1   Major washout
The Coldwater River has washed away 120 metres of the railbed. Unfortunately, there is no easy way around this washout. There is an indistinct trail that goes up through the trees and around the washed-out area. This trail is impassable with a bike. Climbing down the railbed to the riverbed and squezing between the cliff and the river can be done with some difficulty during low stream levels.

13.9   Major washout part two
Sequel to km 13.1.

15.5   Locked gate
An eight foot-high gate and fence impedes travel on the railbed. There is a one-way animal gate 400 metres south along the fence.

15.8   Juliet Station |1005 🏠 🎒 } 🚲 0.8
There is very little evidence of Juliet Station, the site being destroyed by the construction of the highway. The original railgrade runs across the highway at this point. There is no way to get through the highway fences in order to follow the railbed.

16.2   Coquihalla Highway (Exit 240) ⵗ ⵗ
The KVR crosses the Coquihalla Highway, which cannot be followed, but a small detour through an underpass reconnects back on to the right-of-way on the other side of the highway. The Coldwater River Provincial Park Road, from the Coquihalla Highway, turns on to the original KVR right-of-way to the Coldwater River Provincial Park. Following south, you find the picnic area and an information sign that describes Andrew McCulloch's work on the Kettle Valley Railway.

16.4   July Creek 🚶)(
This bridge is now part of the Coldwater River Provincial Park Road.

18.2   KVR railbed disappears under highway ⵗ➔
Continuing south 350 metres on the 4x4 road after leaving the railbed is a one-way animal gate that gives access to the highway.

22.2   Railbed emerges from under the highway but there is no break in the fence to gain access.

22.8   Mine Creek Bridge ✘
Creekbed is easily crossed during dry periods.

Kettle Valley Railway - Coquihalla Subdivision
km 24.9 - km 47.9

23.1 Mine Creek Road (Exit 231) �ʈ ⊱←

From the Coquihalla Highway, turn off on to Mine Creek Road. This road heads south atop the original KVR grade to cross under the highway at km 25.9. Note: there is no exit off the highway from the south nor is there an on ramp heading south at Mine Creek Road. The railbed can be followed back to km 22.8 but no access to the highway has been found there.

26.2 Short detour

The KVR runs into the high fence along the highway. Less then 100 metres down the trail to the south are the twin highway bridges and the KVR bridge that span the Coldwater River. The highway bridges can be walked under to regain the railway at the north end of the KVR bridge.

26.4 Coldwater River)(

The KVR loops briefly across the Coquihalla Highway. The old railway bridge still exists as a road bridge on Exit 228 on the west side of the highway.

26.6 Coquihalla Lakes Exit (Exit 228) �`ᵼ` 🐾

The KVR heads back across to the other side of the highway. Take the overpass across to the other side to reconnect to the railbed. The railbed is used because the north on-ramp of the highway road comes from the Coquihalla Highway to the Coquihalla Summit Provincial Recreation Area, turning onto the KVR to get to the rest area. The Coquihalla Summit Provincial Recreation Area is found beside the right-of-way.

27.6 Britton Creek Rest Area 🐾 🛆 🍴

Rest area with indoor shelter, washrooms and a seasonal concession stand.

27.8 Coquihalla wye. Y

28.9 Coquihalla Lakes Lodge. ⋀ ⌂

29.0 Coquihalla Station ⌇1115 📞 🛆 ⌇ 🚲2.0

Both the station and water tower foundations can be found along the east side of the railbed, beside Coquihalla Lakes.

Tunnel #1 at km 31.7.

Snowshed #15, high above the Coquihalla River, is one of the few sheds still intact, km 45.4.

30.2 Gate

This is the beginning of the Transmountain Pipeline Road. This road travels along the same route as the railway; the road bed is atop the KVR at some points and branches away at others. The road reconnects with the Coquihalla Highway at km 54.5.

Note: The Department of Forestry cautions travellers to watch for rock slides and debris on this road.

31.7 Tunnel #1 ◼66 ⊦→

The pipeline road branches from the railbed just prior to a 66 metre-long tunnel. The railbed is impassable past this point to km 43.8.

32.0 Tunnel #2. ◼85

32.7 Tunnel #3 ◼55

Just below tunnel #3 is the first of three major washouts of the Transmountain Pipeline Road. Each of the washouts is increasingly more difficult to get around. The third washout is nearly impossible. Flanking along the loose rock cliffs around each of the washouts is very dangerous, even more so when carrying a bike. Detour on the Coquihalla Highway at Exit 228 for those not willing to risk life and limb.

32.8 Major washout of road below railgrade.

32.9 Major washout of road below railgrade

Extremely difficult washout to get around. The railbed was washed off the canyon cliffs years ago leaving only the tunnels as reminders that a railway once hung tenuously on the bluffs above.

Baily Bridge across the Coquihalla River 500 metres farther down the road has been washed away. The river can be forded at low stream levels. Past the missing bridge the road is passable.

33.1 Frame trestle. ⋇46

33.3 Frame trestle ⋇123

On September 28, 1969, as part of a demolition exercise by the Canadian Armed Forces, this trestle was blown up.

34.1 Falls Lake Creek ⋇123

Falls Creek Trestle can be seen across the Coquihalla River from the pipeline road. The white lace of Bridalveil Falls and the rugged rock walls provide a dramatic backdrop for the deck lattice girder bridge and frame trestle approaches. The year 1996 was unkind to this bridge as the northern approach has collapsed.

34.5 Tack Creek ⋇96

Frame trestle replaced by steel in 1954—the steel trestle towers remain.

35.8 Filled 89 metre-long frame trestle.

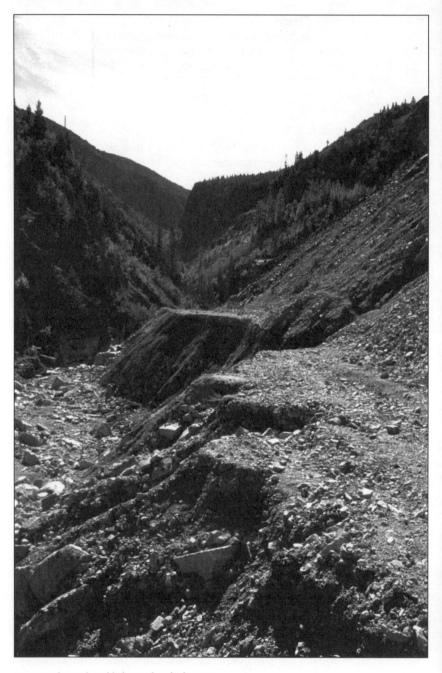

Major washout of road below railgrade, km 32.8.

36.2   Tunnel #4—collapsed ◼76
The line was diverted around this tunnel in 1959 after a slide blocked the entrance.

36.5   Frame trestle. ✕192

37.2   Tunnel #5—collapsed. ◼93

37.3   Frame trestle. ✕41

37.5   Frame trestle. ✕59

37.8   Tunnel #6—collapsed. ◼67

37.9   Romeo water tower. ▮

38.0   Frame trestle. ✕101

38.8   Romeo Station. ▮924 🚂 ⸾ 🚲2.1

41.5   Needle Creek ✕98
The bridge construction used to cross this creek was a through arch span on concrete towers with 15 and 18 metre deck lattice girder approaches. This was the longest clear span on the KVR, at a length of 98 metres. In 1981, the bridge was dismantled for its steel.

43.8   Pipeline road rejoins KVR grade. ⸾←

44.4   Tunnel #7 ◼50
The road passes through this steel-lined tunnel.

45.4   Snowshed #15
The road passes around this 98 metre-long concrete snowshed. Originally, 15 snowsheds existed between km 38.3 and km 45.4, but with improved snow removal equipment, only five of the snowsheds remained during the final operation of this line.

45.5   A rock retaining wall can be found here. Like many others along the KVR, these walls were constructed by stone masons, who fitted the stones without the use of mortar. This mortar-free construction enabled water to drain between the stones, rather than build up a pressure that could possibly overturn the wall.

47.1   Iago water tower. ▮

47.6   Iago Station. ▮739 🚂 ⸾ 🚲2.1

49.8   Pipeline road leaves KVR grade ⸾→
The KVR past this point is overgrown and passage is difficult.

Kettle Valley Railway - Coquihalla Subdivision
km 44.0 - 67.3

49.9   Frame trestle. ✝37

51.5   Deck plate girder bridge. ✝49

52.5   Pipeline road rejoins KVR grade. ⊦←

54.5   Boston Bar Creek Bridge ✝106 Υ ⊦→

A 24 metre deck plate girder with 46 and 36 metre-long frame trestle approaches. Foundations are all that's left to find.

The pipeline road branches from the railbed at this point and follows one of the arms of the Portia Station wye as it heads up the side of Boston Bar Creek. The road then connects with the Coquihalla Highway at the Portia Exit (Exit 202). The highway must then be followed south, as the KVR can not be reaccessed until Carolyn Mines Road at km 61.6.

55.3   Portia Station ⎮584 ◼ ⎬ ⎮ 🚲2.2

An oval sign, with the picture of a steam engine and the station name "Portia," can be found on the Coquihalla Highway acknowledging the historic Kettle Valley Railway and the close proximity of the Portia Station site to the Coquihalla Highway. The KVR crosses the highway at this point and it is difficult, if not impossible, to follow because highway construction has obliterated most of the right-of-way. As the highway heads downhill toward Hope the remains of a ledge that was the KVR can be seen on the hillside.

The wye at this station was primarily used for turning snowplows that operated on this slide prone section between here and Coquihalla Station. The heavy snow conditions of the Coquihalla made this section the most difficult to manage in the winter. The KVR utilized rotary plows, wing plows, 15 snowsheds and numerous men with shovels. The rotary plows were often ineffective, as the snowslides usually contained rock and trees that could destroy the cutting blades. With the advent of bulldozers for snow removal, the CPR was able to eliminate all but five of the original snowsheds.

56.7   Frame trestle ✝34
Filled in 1954.

57.5   Frame trestle. ✝100

59.1   Tunnel #8—collapsed ◼56

Just east of the highway bridge over Ladner Creek there is a trail that leads up the hillside to the railbed and the east portal of the tunnel. A mining exploration crew in 1996 has built a rough trail over the tunnel. The railbed after the bridge to the Carolyn Mines Road is impassable as it is overgrown and washed out in places. With all the activity in the area in mining and forestry this may change, as it has from Carolyn Mines Road to Jessica.

59.2   Ladner Creek Bridge)(170

The last spike ceremony was held near the east end of Ladner Creek
Bridge. The Coquihalla Subdivision was officially opened on July 31,
1916. While following the highway across Ladner Creek, the Ladner
Creek Bridge can be seen up the creek to the northwest.

59.4   Frame trestle.)(41

59.5   Pile trestle.)(14

59.7   Twenty Mile Creek—deck plate girder.)(40

61.6   Tangent Creek)(89

Filled in 1956 and washed out November 24th, 1959. The washout of
this filled-in trestle was never repaired and contributed to the Coquihalla Subdivision's demise.

61.7   Aurum Station—Carolyn Mines Road ¡444 🚂 ͳ 🚲1.9 ¦⟵

An oval sign on the highway marks the close proximity of the Aurum Station site to the Coquihalla Highway. The grade can be found
by taking the Caroline Mines Exit and following it up a short, steep
climb to where the two cross. South, the railbed has been reclaimed
as a road to Jessica.

61.9   Frame trestle.)(13

62.7   Fifteen Mile Creek—frame trestle)(68

The bridge was replaced when the railbed was rebuilt as a road. The
bridge deck is made of two CN flat cars laid side by side.

63.4   Pile trestle.)(55

63.7   Snowshoe Creek—frame trestle.)(110

64.0   Jessica Station   ¡398 🚂 🍴 ¦ 🚻 🚲1.8 ¦➔

An oval sign on the highway marks the close proximity of the Jessica
Station site to the Coquihalla Highway. The site of Jessica Station can
be found by leaving the highway at the turnoff into the Coquihalla River
Recreation Area. This recreation area is composed of 100 hectares for
picnicking, fishing and day use. The KVR right-of-way marks the west
boundary of this recreation area. The station foundation can be found
alongside of the railbed. Past Jessica the railbed again becomes overgrown. A dirt road leaves the railbed just past Jessica and connects to
the pipeline road. South, the pipeline road jumps back on the railbed
for a short distance before the railbed runs under the highway.

64.7   Frame trestle.)(32

64.8   Frame trestle.)(110

65.2   Frame trestle. ⋊73

65.8   Frame trestle. ⋊14

65.9   Coquihalla Highway ↑
        The railbed lies mostly under the grade of the highway from this point
        until km 74.6. There is no access to the KVR at this intersection.

68.4   Eleven Mile Creek—frame trestle. ⋊89

69.2   Pile trestle ⋊14
        The beginning of the end occurred here on November 23, 1959. It had been
        raining hard the last two days so when the call came in that a washout had
        occurred north of Lear, it was not an unusual occurrence. After all, this
        was the Coquihalla and washouts were the norm. Repair crews were dis-
        patched and a work train headed south from Brookmere. On arriving, it
        was discovered that not just one washout had occurred, but four separate
        major washouts had happened. While the immensity of the damage
        swamped the small army of workers, work started immediately on repair-
        ing the washouts. The next day another major washout happened at Tan-
        gent Creek. Up and down the line dozens of washouts took out the railbed
        that week. All told, the damage to the line exceeded $250,000. Work to
        repair and improve the line continued till winter forced a halt until spring.
        But spring did not see a renewed continuance in the work. The Coquihalla
        Canyon fell quiet. On January 9th, 1961, the CPR announced that because
        of the cost of repairs, the decision had been made to abandon the line, so
        the fate of the Coquihalla Subdivision was sealed. The rails and ties were
        removed. Nature took care of the rest.

69.3   Ten Mile Creek—filled frame trestle. ⋊37

72.7   Lear Station |238 🚂 ⤋ 🚴1.0
        An oval sign on the highway marks the close proximity of the Lear
        Station site to the Coquihalla Highway. Lear Station was situated on
        the south side of the aerial tramway, but highway construction has re-
        moved any trace of the site.

74.6   Coquihalla Highway—Othello Road ⊩ Δ ⊢←
        The KVR can be reaccessed by turning off the Coquihalla Highway (Exit 183)
        on to Othello Road toward the Coquihalla Canyon Provincial Recreation
        Area (Quintette Tunnels). Othello Road runs atop the original grade to the
        Provincial Recreation Area. Following the recreation area road keeps you on
        top of the KVR. An information plaque is found just after exiting the high-
        way. It describes the engineering achievement of Andrew McCulloch in the
        construction of the Quintette Tunnels. Othello Tunnels Campground is also
        found along this road, just a short distance from the tunnels.

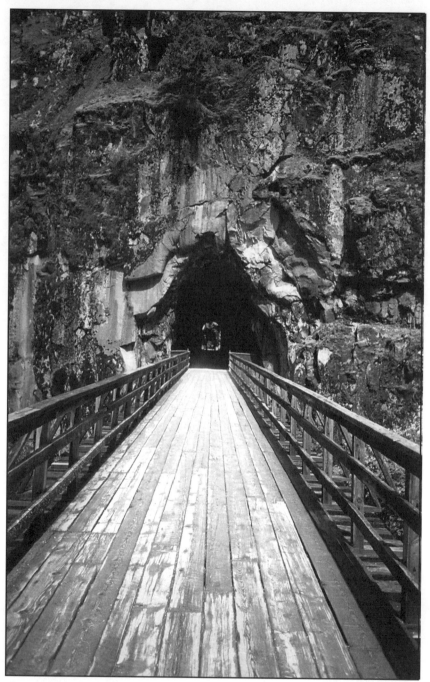

The Quintette Tunnels at Othello, km 78.7, were cut in tangent alignment despite the twisting nature of the narrow Coquihalla Canyon.

78.7 **Othello Station** ǁ176 🚈 ⑂ ⊼ ⁑ 🚲1.5

Less than 10 kilometres from Hope, McCulloch faced a near impossible challenge. The Coquihalla River had cut a horseshoe path through a 91 metre-deep, straight-walled, narrow canyon. There was barely enough room for the river, and certainly no extra room for a railway. Confronted with this challenge, McCulloch and several fellow engineers surveyed the canyon from small woven baskets suspended down into the canyon by ropes from the cliff tops above. After several weeks, McCulloch engineered a perfect tangent alignment of tunnels, later known as the Quintette Tunnels.

In the fall of 1981, the area from Hope to Othello became the site for the filming of the movie *Rambo-First Blood.* The Coquihalla Canyon around the Quintette Tunnels (known as Chapman Gorge in the movie) is where Rambo (Sylvester Stallone) clung for his life on the rock walls above the rushing waters of the Coquihalla River.

Although called the "Quintette" tunnels, there are actually only four as the third tunnel was partially "day-lighted," giving the illusion of five. This section of the KVR through the narrow Coquihalla Canyon has been designated as the Coquihalla Canyon Provincial Recreation Area.

79.6 Tunnel #10 ◼200

Although Tunnel #9 was originally planned, it was never constructed.

79.7 Tunnel #11. ◼30

79.8 Coquihalla River)(23

It's hard to believe, but each autumn salmon struggle against the torrent meltwaters that funnel through this narrow gorge to find their way to spawning grounds.

79.9 Tunnel #12 ◼123

This tunnel is partially open—"day-lighted"—on its north side, creating the illusion of actually being two tunnels.

80.0 Coquihalla River.)(53

80.1 Tunnel #13 ◼101

Past the last tunnel, this next section is incredibly refreshing, not just for the excellent railbed and the welcome downhill grade, but as you cycle, the sights and smells of heavy coastal vegetation envelop you.

80.6 Nicola Valley Trail. 🚶

84.3 Kawkawa Lake Road ⵜ ⑂➔

Kawkawa was a former flagstop on the Kettle Valley Railway. The Kawkawa Lake Road intersecting the KVR can be followed west into Hope. Following the road east will lead you back to Othello. The railbed is only a trail past this point for a short distance before intersecting with Union Bar Road, where it then becomes impassable. You then have to follow Union Bar Road, south, back to Kawkawa Lake Road.

169

85.4   Union Bar Road. ⍏

85.9   Coquihalla River ⅄115 ⛺

As you follow Kawkawa Lake Road into Hope, you first cross the Coquihalla River. Immediately after crossing the river a picnic site is on the north, and Coquihalla Campsite, a large campsite with many services, is on the south.

87.4 Hope Station |44 🚂 ♦ ▷ Y ⚠ ⛪ ⛩ ♦ (🔄 0.3

Just as at Penticton, many locomotives were based at Hope to be used primarily in "helper" service on the heavy grade up through the Coquihalla Pass. This was basically the terminus of the Coquihalla Subdivision, with the remaining line constructed in order to connect to the CPR main line.

Little evidence remains of the once active station at Hope. The railway is not easily found or followed. What you will still find is the original VV&E railway station that was built in 1916 by the Great Northern Railway. Over the years it served as a station for the Canadian National Railway. In 1985, the abandoned building was moved from its site at the corner of Hudson Bay Street and Fifth Avenue to the junction of Highways #1 and #3, now called the Rainbow Junction. The station retains its original look, but now houses a restaurant, a retail outlet and Hope's art centre. This is the last train station of its design in existence.

🚂 Hope Museum 🚃
(919 Water Avenue, 869-7322)

Past Hope there is not much left of the original KVR. The only section that can be cycled is a short 700 metre-long section from Lanstrom Road back to the Fraser River Bridge.

88.0 Fraser River Bridge ✕ 290

This bridge consists of four 72.5 metre-long, double-deck through truss spans, making the total length 290 metres. The upper deck is still being used by motorized vehicles crossing the Fraser River. The lower deck was used by the Kettle Valley Railway to cross the Fraser River and connect to the CPR main line at Odlum. The cross ties of the lower deck have been removed and the bridge barricaded with a fence.

88.9 Lanstrom Road Ƴ

Thick coastal plant life envelops the KVR from Lanstrom Road back to the Fraser River Bridge, turning the right-of-way into a beautiful tree-covered lane. West from Lanstrom Road, plant life has reclaimed the KVR where land developers have yet to remove the grade for housing projects.

91.1 Odlum Station |55

Odlum was originally named Petain after a World War I French army hero, but in 1940 was renamed Odlum after the head of Canada's overseas forces. It was decided to change the name after Petain sided with the pro-Nazis. Odlum was the terminal point of the KVR track, connecting the KVR main line with the CPR main line. The Canadian Pacific Railway main line continues to Vancouver. 🚂

Columbia & Western Railway
Castlegar to Midway
162.3 km

Columbia & Western Railway (C&W)
(Boundary Pathway)
Castlegar to Midway, 162.3 kilometres

The C&W was originally chartered in 1896 by Fritz Heinze, with the objective to ensure a reliable connection between his smelter in Trail and the markets, without having his hands tied by either Daniel Corbin with the Spokane Falls & Northern Railway or the Columbia & Kootenay Steam & Navigation Company. His planned route was to Penticton, but if dissatisfied with the connection there to the CPR, he planned to take his railway to the coast. In spite of his grand plans, Heinze sold the C&W to CPR in 1898. CPR started construction from Castlegar in 1898, reaching Grand Forks in September of 1899. By 1900 the line reached Midway, with a spur line from Eholt to Phoenix, and a spur from Eholt to the Emma mine. A branch line was built to Deadwood, running behind the smelter at Anaconda. In 1992 the line was abandoned and the tracks removed.

Cycling the C&W is a spectacular experience. The right-of-way hangs on mountainsides and boundless vistas spread out below your wheels. Long tunnels and huge rock retaining walls help to keep the railbed glued to the cliffs. Views of Lower Arrow Lake and Christina Lake seem to go on forever. This is a trip that takes you far off the beaten path and into the wilderness. Between the three major centres, Castlegar, Grand Forks and Midway, the railbed does not follow the same valleys as the roads, thus leading the cyclist into backcountry not normally ventured into. This has to be taken into account before riding this railway, as there are very few access points along most of the C&W.

Starting at the C&W Station in downtown Castlegar, you find that the tracks remain and are still in use from the Castlegar Station to km 8.8. From km 8.8, the railway climbs at a grade greater than 2% to the summit at Farron. En route to Farron, the railway passes through the 916 metre-long Bull Dog Tunnel, connecting Pup Creek and Dog Creek valleys.

From Farron, the C&W follows the narrow McRae Creek Canyon down to Christina Lake. The creek is falling faster than the railway, and leaves the railbed high on the canyon wall. In a downhill rush the railway finally bottoms out at Cascade, where it begins a slow climb to Grand Forks. The railbed is in great shape until Cascade, where it turns up the Kettle River Valley and becomes increasingly overgrown. Depending on the time of year, it may not be passable.

Past Grand Forks, the C&W continues to climb to Eholt before descending into Midway. Although the railbed to Eholt is in excellent shape, the section from Eholt to Midway is starting to become overgrown in spots. Most of the problem areas are adjacent to pasture land and access has been restricted to motorized traffic ▰

Columbia & Western Railway
km 0.0 – 17.3

Castlegar Station has been restored and serves as Castlegar's museum, km 0.0.

km   **Castlegar Station** ⱶ*439* 🚂 📖 🍴 ⩔ ⵉ 🛆 🏛 ⊓ 🔋 🚻 🚲 *0.9* ⱶ→
0.0   In 1902, the CPR completed a railway bridge across the Columbia River enabling the rail-lines to be linked between the Columbia and Kootenay, the Columbia and Western, and the Kettle Valley railways. Thus began the history of Castlegar.

    Although the original station burned to the ground in 1906, it was immediately replaced and remains one of the best preserved in the province. The station at Castlegar was moved from the middle of the wye intersection 100 metres east, to the corner of 13th Avenue and 3rd Street. Restored, it now serves as the Castlegar Museum. A detour down Arrow Lakes Drive to km 8.8 is required to bypass the still active section of the railway.

IMPORTANT NOTICE

At the time of writing (spring 1997), the railbed from Castlegar to Grand Forks is the property of Canadian Pacific Limited (CPR). Presently, the Trans Canada Trail Foundation and local rails-to-trails organizations are in the process of trying to come to an agreement with the CPR for the transfer of this right-of-way to public lands. Until such a transfer, anyone who enters on to this railbed without CPR's express permission is trespassing. The inclusion of this section in this book is not intended to promote the use of CPR's property but is only preparatory to the transfer of these lands to public hands. Before venturing on to this right-of-way check with the Outdoor Recreation Council of B.C. as to the ownership status of the railbed.

Columbia & Western Railway
km 17.1 - 49.6

___

⬛▬ ▬⬛ Castlegar Museum ▬⬛ ⬛▬
13th Ave. & 3rd St., 365-6440

___

2.6   Robson West Station |430 🚂 ‖ 🚲 1.0

Robson West was the terminus of Heinze's C&W from Trail. Barges would ferry the train up Lower Arrow Lake to connect to the CPR.

3.8   Kraft Station 🚂 |/

This station came into existence when the Celgar Pulp Mill was built.

7.1   Westley Station 🚂

In 1964, a revision in the railway at this point was required owing to the construction of the Hugh Keenleyside Dam. The revision moved 5.6 kilometres of the line higher onto the hillside, bypassing the former station of Labarthe and the Labarthe Tunnel.

8.2   Arrow Lakes Drive ⌐

A small side road leads along the tracks to their end.

8.8   Locked gate across right-of-way—end of side road |←

Access the railbed here. From here to km 10.1 the rails are still in place, but are now filled in with ballast.

10.1   End of ballast-filled rails

Loose ballast from the end of the rails to km 16.3 makes cycling difficult. As you climb the rail grade your views of Lower Arrow Lake will be of numerous log booms and a few tug boats awaiting their turn for the Celgar Pulp Mill.

11.6   Labarthe Tunnel ⬛57

The current line bypasses the tunnel, which is submerged under Lower Arrow Lake during spring run off. Labarthe Station, at km 11.0 on the bypassed line, utilized a turntable for turning around helper engines that were required for the steep grade to Farron.

Columbia & Western Railway Profile

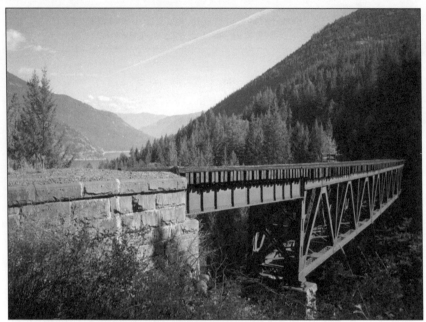

Extensive rock work is a common site along this subdivision, be it trestle approach or retaining walls.

As you follow the railbed from Castlegar along Lower Arrow Lake you begin to climb and the views become spectacular.

14.9 Washout
A single track path up to the south skirts around this 50 metre-long washout. As you follow the railbed you can't help but notice how for most of the way from Castlegar to Cascade you hang upon the cliff as the valley seems to get farther and farther below. Helping to hold the railway on to the cliff are extensive rock retaining walls. Many of these massive walls are constructed of granite, finely crafted by Italian stone masons.

16.3 Loose ballast ends.

16.8 McCormack Creek Bridge)(125x58
Five deck plate girders carried the railway over McCormack Creek.

21.2 Shields Creek Forest Service Road ✝
Thirteen kilometres south on this road connects to Highway #3 400 metres east of the junction of Highways #3 and #3A.

21.5 Shields Station |609 🚂 ⛟ ♪ 🚲2.1
A large open area is all that is left of Shields Station.

22.6 Tunnel. ⬛50

23.6 Tunnel. ⬛118

24.8 Farr Creek)(102
A 65 metre-long through truss with deck plate approaches crosses Farr Creek.

25.6 Cub Creek—deck plate girders.)(125

27.6 Coykendahl Tunnel ⬛89
Enter this tunnel a little cautiously as the curvature makes for total blackness in the centre, and the railbed gets a little rough in places.

28.1 Coykendahl siding. ♪

28.7 Coykendahl Station |778 🚂 🚲1.3
A tuscan red shed built into the side of the hill remains at this station.

29.0 Coykendahl water tower. ⛟

31.2 Rockfall
A narrow path leads through this 40 metre-long rockfall.

33.0 Small rockfall.

36.6 Major washout
Narrow single track on top of what's left of a large fill that spans a tributary of Brooklyn Creek.

Columbia & Western Railway
km 49.2 - 74.4

38.2   A small 4x4 road follows Brooklyn Creek down to the town site of Brooklyn.

Brooklyn

In the spring of 1898, William Parker's mining claim opposite Deer Park on the shores of Lower Arrow Lake became the construction headquarters of the C&W. In the three months of June, July and August, the town of Brooklyn came to life. By September, Brooklyn boasted 16 hotels, a hospital and stores supplying goods from boots to wholesale liquor. But before the year had ended the residents and businesses were leaving Brooklyn in droves for greener pastures farther down the line. By the next summer Brooklyn was little more than a ghost town.

38.4   Bulldog Tunnel ▮912

During the construction of this tunnel, a series of switchbacks carried the line over the top of the tunnel. Over a distance of 8.2 kilometres, a 4% grade up six legs of switchbacks took the trains up 155 metres to the summit, then a 4% grade down six legs of switchbacks brought the trains back down 123 metres to reconnect with the line. Today, there is little evidence of the switchbacks. The tunnel itself cuts a straight line from east to west with a slight hook at the west end. Travelling from west to east is preferable because once around the corner you just walk toward the light at the other end, but coming from the east you walk in total darkness for almost the total length of the tunnel. The east end of the tunnel almost always has water cascading down the side of the entrance.

39.7   Tunnel Station ¦980 ▰ ¦ ☎1.9

The station foundation can still be found, as well as an apple tree overlooking Dog Creek Valley. This spot would make a reasonable campsite except for the absence of a reliable water source.

41.1   Water tank. ☗

41.2   Quinn Creek

A large fill crosses the creek.

42.3   Dog Creek Trail—Peter Lake Trail ☖

Dog Creek Trail follows along the shore of Cog Creek and reconnects with the railbed at km 49.9. Peter Lake Trail leaves Cog Creek Trail at the confluence of Peter Creek and Dog Creek and follows Peter Creek for eight kilometres to a beautiful lake surrounded by steep mountainsides.

46.6   Porcupine Creek

The large curved trestle that originally spanned this canyon was later replaced by fill when upgraded by the CPR.

49.9   Water flows have carved channels in the railbed.

50.9   Dog Creek Trail ☖

East portal of the 912 metre-long Bulldog Tunnel, km 38.4.

51.6   Farron Station |1212 🚂 ⬤ ♦ Y 🚴1.8

Named after one of the railway construction engineers, Farron was the summit station of the Monashee Mountains and a turning point for helper locomotives. Along with the station house, the foundations of three other residences can be discovered here. The most prominent remaining item is the concrete diesel cistern alongside the railbed.

53.0   Bomb monument

At this spot in 1924 a bomb planted on a passenger train exploded, killing nine people including Peter Verigin, leader of the Doukhobors. A small monument remains west of and adjacent to the railbed.

55.5   Mount Gladstone Trail. 🏃

57.3   Bonanza siding—Paulson Detour Road Ⴤ

Paulson Detour Road accesses Highway #3.

59.3   Paulson Station |1074 🚂 ♦ ⬤B X̄B 🚴1.4

As work on the railway moved to Grand Forks, the Paulson Brothers established a hotel, store and stables here. Once the railway was completed, the hotel sitting alongside the railway became known as Paulson Station. Later a siding was added at km 57.3 to service ore shipments from the Bonanza mine and the station was sometimes referred to as Bonanza Siding. A stone foundation and the remains of other buildings along the banks of McRae Creek can be found.

The flat valley bottom alongside the railbed, with McRae Creek meandering through it, makes the area around Paulson a beautiful spot to set up a backcountry campsite.

60.9   Highway #3 Overpass

There is no access to the highway at this point, as the highway bridge passes high above the rail grade.

61.3   Paulson Tunnel. ▣111

63.1   Rock retaining wall—another of the numerous retaining walls along this stretch of the Columbia & Western Railway.

64.5   Water tower. ⬤

65.7   Coryell Station |968 🚂 ⬤ ♦ 🚴2.2

The town of Coryell was founded in 1898 under the name of Gladstone. Gladstone sprung up from the news that the construction on the railway had begun at Castlegar and that Gladstone would be one of the stations on route. The railway was not the only reason for the town. Burnt Basin, about two kilometres from the town site, had been staked by miners as early as 1896. News of the possible mining riches in the area contributed to the influx of miners to the area at the same time the railway was being constructed.

4c

Columbia & Western Railway

km 72.6 - 100.3

N

Christina

Texas Point

English Point

Lake

Stewart

Creek

72.6

Lafferty

76.5

Christina

77.2

Baker Cr

79.7

82.0

Fife

Sutherland

82.2

MOUNT MORRISSEY

Spooner Cr

Christina Lake

84.5

84.8

Moody

Christina

86.8

Creek

98.4

Billings

91.7

91.8

Cascade

89.1

90.2

89.6

Gilpin

Gilpin Creek

Kettle

River

BNR

At its height the town boasted four hotels, three general stores, a restaurant and bakery, livery stables and a dance hall. In the summer of 1899 the town's population jumped as track layers came through town, but by the beginning of 1900 the town had shrunk to one hotel and the railway station. On January 8, 1900, the station was renamed Coryell after John A. Coryell, the engineer who made the first surveys for a coast-to-Kootenay line.

Today little remains of the town except the station foundations and a red railway shed sitting off to the side of the railbed.

70.8   Snowslide bridge.)(41

72.6   Lafferty Station ¡820 🚈 ⌡ ⱴ ⤢2.2

Lafferty Station was named for a Rossland bank manager.

73.0   Lafferty Road Ⲭ

Lafferty Road makes a steep climb down to Highway #3.

73.1   Lafferty water tower. 🏮

76.5   Christina

Christina was a former flagstop named for Christina Lake. Large concrete rock retaining wall overlooks English Cove on Christina Lake.

79.7   Water tower 🏮

Concrete foundation blocks remain.

82.0   Wooden ore bin for a large lime quarry here at Fife. ✂

82.2   Fife Station ¡599 🚈 🏮 ⱴ Ⲭ ⛰ ⌂ 🏮 ⑂ 🍴 ⚫ ⤢1.9

A small tuscan red section shed serves to mark the location of Fife. Two six foot-high fences line Fife Road with pedestrian walk throughs.

Christina Lake

NOT TO SCALE

Looking out to Christina Lake, km 76.0.

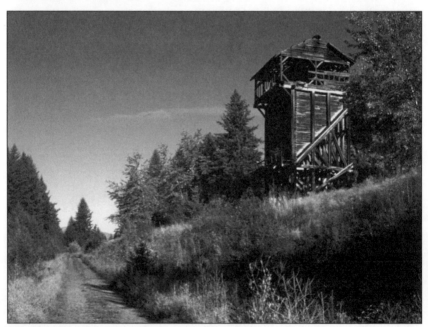

A wooden ore bin for a large lime quarry at Fife, km 82.0.

Unfortunately, a bike will not fit through the openings. Bikes have to be tossed over the fences. Past Fife, the railbed becomes increasingly weedy, although the high traffic volume of cyclists from Christina Lake usually keeps twin tracks clear through the weeds.

1.9 steep, downhill kilometres on Fife Road will take you to Highway #3 and Christina Lake where most amenities can be found. Across the intersection of Fife Road and Highway #3 is Wildways Adventure Sports and Tours, which is the local bicycle repair shop. If you don't feel like tackling the steepness of Fife Road on the return journey, take Santa Rosa Road, 1.6 kilometres south on Highway #3, which is not quite as steep.

86.5   Water tank 🚰 ⸗

A four-car siding was situated here.

86.8   Santa Rosa Road—Dewdney Trail ⸸ 🏛 ⸗

The overpass that was here was removed in 1992 and replaced with a fill. A slight detour around the west side of the fill is required to reconnect to the railbed. Santa Rosa Road connects with Highway #3 and the town site of Christina, 1.3 kilometres down the hill.

The historic Dewdney Trail also crosses the railbed at this point, although mostly overgrown sections of it east of the railbed can be ridden. Refer to Mike Wisnicki's *Over the Hill* for more information.

89.1   Kettle River.)(154

89.6   Cascade wye. Y

90.2   **Cascade Station** |463 🏠 ⸸ 🚲0.5 ⸗⇒

Highway #395 crosses the C&W at the site of the former Cascade Station. Past Cascade, the railbed becomes increasingly overgrown with weeds as it enters Grand Forks.

Cascade was known as "The Gateway City" and considered unique because it owed its existence to water power. The booming mines of the Boundary district needed electricity; it was the availability of a hydroelectric power supply that sustained the dreams of this community for so many years. However, its birth must still be credited to the Columbia & Western Railway.

As with many of the turn-of-the-century boom towns, Cascade also met its demise, and today only a couple of homes remain with most of the 17-hotel town site converted into a golf course. The powerhouse remains standing yet abandoned, a symbol of a town of such promise for the future.

91.7   Kettle River—deck truss with deck plate girder approaches.)(52

91.8   **Billings** ⸸

Billings was a flag stop on the railway and the site of the Yale Columbia Sawmill. Past Billings the railbed gets increasingly weedy, except for those sections that the local farmers use as access roads to their fields.

Columbia & Western Railway
km 100.3 - 131.4
Kettle River Valley Railway
km 0.0 - 18.4
V V & E Phoenix Subdivision
km 0.0 - 3.8

5c

Hodges

THIMBLE MTN. TRAILS

Troutdale

Fisherman Cr

Niagara

Caesar

Fisherman

Creek

Sand

North Fork Road

(KRVR)

Granby

Granby

Granby Smelter

Copper Jct

Westend

Grand Forks

W&E

Kettle

Cuprum

Carson

KRVR

River

98.4 Gilpin Station ¡507 🚉 ⫦ 🔭0.1
Named after the first customs agent in the area.

103.1 Collins Road. ⫯

105.4 White Hall Road. ⫯

106.6 Nursery Road. ⫯

107.1 Kettle River—through truss and half deck plate girder spans.)(70

107.4 Darcy Road ⫯ ⫦→
Darcy Road creates a deep cut in the fill. On the other side of the road
the rails are still in and are actively being used by the Burlington Northern Railroad. Detour south on Darcy, west on Cameron, north on
Kenmore, east on Sagamore Avenue, north on International, which immediately turns into 2 Street and crosses the Kettle River. From there
turn east on 72 Avenue, south on 8 Street and then west on Kettle River
Drive. Pick up the railway again just as Kettle River Drive turns south.

108.9 Cuprum—Kettle River Valley Railway junction.

110.0 Kettle River)(83
The active railway and the rails end at the east end of the bridge.

The rock retaining wall holds the C&W high on the mountainside above Christina Lake, km 85.0.

Grand Forks Station, has now been restored and serves as a neighborhood pub, km 111.3.

110.1 Kettle River Drive. ⵙ ⵙ⟵

110.4 Boundary Drive. ⵙ

110.9 Highway #3 ⵙ

Grand Forks and area is blessed with a myriad of trails for the mountain biker. For more information get hold of the book *Over the Hill* by Mike Wisnicki or ask Larry about the trails at the Silver Barn Bike Shop west on Highway #3.

111.2 76th Avenue.

111.3 Grand Forks Station |523 ⬛🚂 ⵙ Ɏ Ⲩ ⛰ 🏛 🚻 🍎 🍴 🍷 ☕ 🚲1.6 ⵙ⟸

Grand Forks was an early settlement in 1865, the same year that Edgar Dewdney was cutting his famous trail from Hope to Fort Steele. In 1897, the settlement was incorporated as the city of Grand Forks. Other town sites rapidly grew with the discovery of copper at Phoenix and Mother Lode near Greenwood. The Granby Smelter was located at Grand Forks, and was the largest copper smelter in the British Empire. With 20 years of prosperity, farming also developed with many orchards planted. The year 1919 saw a decline in copper and subsequent closure of the smelter. This was a blow to the area, resulting in little growth until seed growing, logging and sawmill operations again brought prosperity back to the community.

🚂 Boundary Museum 🚂
7370 5th St., 442-3737

Many buildings and landmarks can still be found from the town's affluence during the turn of the century. A walking tour guide through historic Grand Forks can be obtained at the Boundary Museum.

As the Columbia & Western Railway could not obtain suitable right-of-way into the city of Grand Forks, its station was actually built in the city of Columbia, now know as West Grand Forks. The station has been beautifully restored and now houses the Grand Forks Station Neighbourhood Pub and Columbia Grill. It is the oldest CPR station in B.C., still in its original location and it is protected under a Heritage Designation Bylaw. Many historical artifacts of the railway can be found adorning the pub's walls, 442-5855.

112.1 Westend—Kettle River Valley Railway junction (KRVR). Ɏ ⵙ

112.4 North Fork Road. ⵙ

112.6 VV&E Phoenix junction.

113.8 Granby—Granby Smelter spur. Ɏ

Columbia & Western Railway
km 130.6 - 144.4
C & W Phoenix Subdivision
km 0.0 - 15.6
V V&E Phoenix Subdivision
km 6.7 - 38.9

6c

117.5   Road ⍦

This 4x4 road connects to North Fork Road down the hill; up the hill it connects with Son Ranch Road, which connects to Highway #3 on the other side of the mountain range.

120.3   Fisherman Station. ⌐679 🚂 🚲*2.1*

121.2   Fisherman Creek Road ⍦

Down the hill the road leads to Niagara and a connection with North Fork Road. Uphill the road leads to Thimble Mountain Trails and Highway #3.

Niagara

Niagara was another railway boom town that popped up because of the C&W. Construction in the town started in the fall of 1898 and peaked by the start of 1899. Before the summer of 1899, the town had already shrunk to half its peak and was declining fast. At its peak it boasted 12 hotels, nine general stores, three butcher shops, a couple of blacksmiths and a host of other businesses. By the end of year there were only a handful of die-hard residents left in Niagara. When construction on the KVR commenced in 1906, Niagara saw a brief resurgence.

121.9   Cattle guard.

122.9   Tuscan red railway maintenance shed is still standing at the south end of the tunnel.

123.0   Tunnel. 🚇*125*

127.6   Tunnel. 🚇*156*

128.2   Hodges Station. 🚂

130.0   Water tower ♟

Concrete foundation still remains.

130.7   Brown Creek Forest Service Road (F.S.R.) ⍦

The railbed is used by logging trucks from this point to Eholt Road, thus turning it into a washboard.

131.9   Brown Creek F.S.R. ⍦

133.1   Cattle guard.

133.3   Eholt water tower. ♟

133.6   Eholt Road. ⍦

133.7   Eholt Station & Phoenix junction ⌐951🚂 ♟ ⌇ ⎥ Y ⍦ 🚲*1.4*

It was back in 1898 that the CPR designated Eholt as a railroad divisional point along the C&W, thus assuring its future as a town site. By 1899, over

Columbia & Western Railway
km 140.2 - 162.3

7c

a hundred lots were sold only two weeks after they went on the market, and some 30 buildings were already in the course of construction. Later that same year Eholt had five hotels, a true symbol of prosperity in this time period. During its prime, Eholt boasted a population of about 300. However, with the collapse of the world copper market following World War I, the demise of Eholt began.

Today, not a single building from the town or the CPR operations remain, only a couple of foundations and some lilac bushes. Three farms now occupy the meadow where the town itself once stood. It is said that at Eholt, even the ghosts have gone.

The access road to Highway #3 from Eholt follows atop the Phoenix Branch Line. This 15.5 kilometre-long branch, abandoned in 1921, climbs steeply up to Phoenix at a 3.4% grade. Although time has taken its toll on pieces of this railbed, it certainly offers a challenge to those willing to tackle it.

134.0   Other branch of the wye.

134.1   Gate

At this point the C&W straddles agricultural land and is cross fenced and gated in numerous places.

137.9   Highway #3 �␣

There are double gates just prior to the highway and a single gate on the other side. The railbed continues to become increasingly weedy except for those sections that have some vehicle traffic on them.

143.2   Private access road to Highway #3. ⱡ

145.2   Highway #3 ⱨ

The original wooden trestle over the highway was later filled in with two concrete tunnels for the highway to pass through the fill at ground level. The fill and tunnels have recently been removed, as the concrete tunnels were in disrepair. A highway tunnel dated 1912 was found in the fill and remains intact for heritage interpretive purposes. Also dated 1912 is a large stone arch culvert for Boundary Creek, found under the railway grade. Although the fill no longer exists, the highway is easily crossed.

145.4   Boundary Creek.

146.5   Spur. ⱶ

147.3   Deadwood / Mother Load Mine spur—Louisa Street ⱶ ⱡ

At the end of this spur line lay the Mother Lode Mine. Although discovered in 1891, it was not until 1896 that the mine was developed. By the end of 1905, 752,431 tonnes of ore had been shipped to the smelter at Anaconda. In 1913, the glory of the Mother Lode came to an end with a monumentous explosion planned to dislodge further ore, but instead it became hazardous and more expensive to work.

During the increasingly prosperous years of the Mother Lode Mine it was thought that the opportunity existed for a new town near the mine site. So was developed the town of Deadwood. Although there was initial enthusiasm, the population never exceeded 100. The majority of miners and their families lived at the mine site, home for about 400 people.

This 8.4 kilometre spur is generally passable with a few overgrown sections as it climbs up the Mother Lode Creek Valley.

147.5 Greenwood Station |762 🚂 🏠 🍴 🏕 ⛺ 🏛 🚹 🍺 (🚲1.0

Greenwood finds its origin back in 1895 when for the price of $5,000, 81 hectares was purchased and development began. Greenwood obtained city status in 1897 and quickly became a bustling mining town with a population of 3,000 by 1899. By the end of 1899, 26 hotels were registered as operating in Greenwood with copper being the main reason for the town's prosperity. It was also in 1899 that the Columbia & Western Railway reached Greenwood, reaping the rewards from the mines in the area. But as with all other surrounding areas, falling demand for ore following World War I was hard on Greenwood. However, the city survived with persistent individuals, and the turning of industry to logging and millwork. Mining of copper resumed again for a period after World War II. Unfortunately, the original station burned down following a train wreck in 1964.

Today, the mines are all closed and with a population of 7,000 the economy depends mainly upon logging. Numerous historical buildings remain from the late 1800s and early 1900s reflecting the affluence of the time. A heritage tour map can be obtained from the Greenwood Museum, enabling one to see Greenwood, B.C.'s smallest city, as it was at the turn of the century.

🚂 Greenwood Museum 🚂
2145 Copper St., 445-6355

148.4 Washington Street. ⛪

148.9 Boundary Creek.)(41

150.1 Boundary Creek.)(21

150.3 Anaconda |735

The smelter at Greenwood was built in 1898 at the mouth of Copper Creek in the town called Anaconda. During its time, the smelter was considered the most modern plant in every respect. The smelter began its operations in 1901, running 24 hours a day. In 1912, production began to slow with decreasing supplies of ore. By 1918 the smelter closed completely. The site was sold to Leon Lotzkar who later gave the site to the city of Greenwood. It is currently known as Lotzkar Park.

Today, you will find many remains of this once active smelter. The smelter smokestack, which was originally made from sheet metal, dates back to 1904 when the metal was replaced with 250,000 bricks and built to the height of 36 metres. You can follow the many walking paths through the mountains of black waste slag that had been loaded into bell-shaped slag cars, then taken by rail to be dumped nearby. Many of the giant hardened black bells that once glowed red in the night can be found within the park. Lotzkar Park can be accessed by turning west on Washington Street, then taking Smelter Road, which follows the Mother Load spur line to the smelter site.

Weeds start to become a major problem after this point. Also, beware that the railbed is ditched at each of the road crossings.

152.0 Boundary Creek Provincial Park Δ ₿

This small campsite is right across the creek. To get there, ford the creek or detour on to Highway #3 at Anaconda or Boltz Road. There is also a small road that touches the railbed at km 151.2, which bridges Boundary Creek.

153.2 Boundary Falls Station ¡706 🚂 ⸱ ⸱ 🚲1.5

Placer gold was discovered in Boundary Creek in 1860 and over the next 15 years various claims were worked sporadically. Renewed interest in the area came in 1887 when a rich supply of quartz was discovered near Boundary Falls. By the time the railway arrived in 1900, the small town of Boundary Falls was bustling with activity. A copper smelter and hydro-electric plant were in the plans, all of which thrived up until 1905.

Today Boundary Falls remains a beautiful place to explore. From a viewpoint a short distance from the railway, you can still see in the cliff above the falls the old wooden dam built in 1900, the concrete support and wooden trestle for the wood stove pipe.

154.1 Boltz Road. ⸸

156.3 Kerr Road. ⸸

162.3 Midway Station ¡580 🚂 ₿ ⸱ Υ Δ 🏠 ₿ (

Midway was the division point between the C&W and the KV railways. The station was designated a heritage building and presently serves as the Midway Museum.

Vancouver, Victoria & Eastern
Phoenix Branch – 38.9 kilometres

Eager to get a piece of the rich Phoenix ore hauling pie, the VV&E reached Phoenix in 1904 after overcoming many obstacles thrown in its path by the C&W and the KRVR. But in March 1905, the line started passenger and freight service out of Phoenix. With maximum grades of 2.2%, less than the maximum grade of 3.4% found on the C&W, the VV&E quickly captured the bulk of the ore shipments out of Phoenix. The fall of copper prices in 1919 ended the existence of Phoenix and the railway. The tracks were all pulled up by 1921.

This 38.9 kilometre-long branch of the VV&E loops south around Eagle Mountain, then north up July Creek to circle up Montezuma Hill to Phoenix. The first 11.6 kilometres of this railway winds around the southern edge of Eagle Mountain and is overgrown and impassable. At km 11.6 Danshine Village Road jumps on to the railbed and follows it to km 16.9. The right-of-way continues past km 16.9 through private property and slowly becomes more overgrown. The next passable section is accessed from Phoenix Road at km 23.2. From here to the missing bridge at Glenside Creek (km 29.1), the railbed is in excellent condition. For the extreme adventurer, bushwhacking past three missing trestles finds the railbed in good condition into Phoenix. Otherwise, a detour up to Marshall Lake and back down Providence Creek Trail will bypass the three missing trestles. Links with the C&W Phoenix Branch and B.C. Copper Company Mine spur gives one lots of options to fill a day or two.

km

0.0   Copper junction. ⅄

0.4   Kettle River Valley Railway crossing.

1.6   Columbia junction. ⅄

1.8   Weston Station. 🏠

3.2   Copper junction. ⅄

5.5   Frame trestle. ⅝174

6.6   Frame trestle. ⅝22

7.0   Reservoir Road. ⅄

7.1   Frame trestle. ⅝12

7.6   Frame trestle. ⅝12

8.7   Frame trestle. ⅝12

4x4 road connects from highway.

10.9   Spur. |/

11.4   Spencer Station. 🚋

11.6   Danshine Village Road |←
This road runs atop the original grade to km 16.9.

14.6   Frame trestle. ⋈107

16.9   Danshine Village Road departs railbed |→
The railbed can be followed, though it slowly becomes increasingly overgrown. Take Highway #3 to Phoenix Road and reconnect with VV&E at km
23.2.

18.6   Highway #3. ⊤

22.8   Fisherman Creek—frame trestle. ⋈30

23.0   Hale Station. 🚋 🛉 ⌡ ⊤

23.2   Phoenix Road ⊤ |←
The railbed is passable from the missing trestle at km 22.8 to the missing trestle over Glenside Creek at km 29.1.

25.3   4x4 road
This 400 metre-long 4x4 road up the hill connects with C&W Phoenix
Branch at km 4.6.

25.4   Denoro Oro Mine. ⚒

25.6   Denoro Station. 🚋 🛉 ⌡ |/

25.7   Columbia and Western Railway interchange |/
Taking the spur down will connect you with the C&W Phoenix branch.

28.5   Glenside Station. 🚋 🛉 ⌡

29.1   Glenside Creek—frame trestle ⋈205x60 |→
There are only a couple of A bends still standing on the other side of the
creek. This trestle and the next three are missing, but the railbed between
them is passable except for a number of fallen trees across the railbed. The
real difficulty is getting through the thick bush in each of the creek valleys.
Getting across Glenside Creek is about as bad as it gets, which is nearly
impossible. To detour, take the steep 4x4 road up to Marshall Lake and
then take Providence Creek Trail to reconnect with the railway at km 34.5.

30.2   Spur. |/

31.2   Frame trestle. ⋈51

31.5   Frame trestle. ✕128

33.4   Marshall Lake Ski Trail intersects railbed.

34.2   Providence Creek Trail ⊢←
        4x4 road bypasses missing trestle.

34.4   Providence Creek. ✕90

34.5   Trestle bypass reconnects.

37.6   Jordan Station. 🚂 ⌷

37.8   Phoenix Road ⊤ ⊢→
        Railbed on the other side of the road quickly becomes lost in the open
        pit mines.

38.8   Granby Victoria Mine spur and wye. ⌵ ⅄

38.9   Phoenix Station 🚂 ⬤ ⌷ ⅄

Phoenix was a mining town built atop a mountain of copper. At an
elevation of 1400 metres, Phoenix was the highest city in Canada. Phoenix was incorporated as a city in 1900 and provided the very best in
accommodations and services. By 1911, about 4,000 people lived in
Phoenix. There was a hospital, tennis courts, moving pictures, a brew-
ery and 17 saloons that stayed open day and night. There was skating,
curling, hockey and skiing. The first professional hockey in British Columbia was played in Phoenix.

For a time Phoenix was the largest producer of copper ore in Canada.
However, by 1919 the company closed the mines due to a depleted
supply, falling prices and an uncertain demand for copper. Railway
service soon slowed and the residents began moving away. By 1920,
Phoenix was a ghost town. In 1955, the Granby Company returned to
the mountain to develop an open pit mine. Over the next 20 years the
pit grew to encompass not only the old mining areas, but all the town
site of Phoenix, leaving little to remain from the old pioneer mining
era. The station location is lost somewhere in the middle of this large
open pit mine.

C&W Phoenix Subdivision
15.6 kilometres

Construction started on the Phoenix Subdivision in 1899 and the last spike was struck on May 21, 1900. Although completed in May, the first load of ore shipped to the Granby Smelter in Grand Forks did not take place until July 11th. With grades approaching 3.4%, Shay engines similar to the one used now by the Kettle Valley Steam Railway were used on the steep grades. In 1905, when the VV&E climbed into Phoenix, it took away the majority of the ore-hauling trade from the C&W because of the easier grades and heavier trains that could be operated on them. The Phoenix mines kept both railways busy until 1919 when post World War I copper prices plumented. The railway was abandoned and the track removed in 1921.

Cycling this subdivision involves an exploration of the mines of the past. The honeycomb mining techniques and the deep pits remain to be explored. Beware: these mines are dangerous places. Most are very deep, steep-sided pits filled with water. It is easy to fall in to one while wandering through the woods. The railbed is almost totally intact and is relatively easy to cycle from Eholt to Phoenix. Three minor detours are required. The first is just out of Eholt after crossing Highway #3. A 60 metre-long section of the railbed is totally overgrown and impassable with a bike. The second detour is at Denoro where the frame trestle over the VV&E Phoenix branch is missing, requiring a detour around Oro Denoro mines and up a 4x4 road to regain the railbed after the missing trestle. The third is at the switchback at Hartford, where the road built upon the old railbed skirts 700 metres around a rock bluff that the railbed made a deep cut through. The railway is somewhat overgrown in this cut, but passable with some difficulty. Once at Phoenix, the railbed totally disappears within the open pit mines.

Options for riding this section are to make circle routes using the VV&E and the Providence Lake Ski trails, taking one railway up and the other back down.

km	Phoenix junction km 134.6 C&W
0.0	

0.3   Highway #3 ⋮→

Fences line both sides of Highway #3. The railbed is difficult to pick up after crossing the highway. It is totally overgrown for the first 60 metres and is impassable by bike. It can be hiked through on foot but not while pushing a bike. There is an old concrete foundation buried in the trees on the east side of the railbed 30 metres past the fence. The railbed can be accessed by bike by taking the rough road just opposite Eholt Road east on Highway #3 and following it to the west. It will connect to the railbed just after the overgrown section.

0.4   4x4 road connects from highway ⋮←

The railbed is rough in a few spots from here to km 1.1.

1.1   Logging road going down

Railbed is in excellent shape after this point.

2.0   Logging road going up.

2.7   Views of Eholt Valley.

3.5   Denoro—B.C. Mines spur

Named B.C. Junction and then Coltern, this station was finally named Denoro when a spur line was built to the Oro Denoro Mine.

Denoro

The spur departs to the west (right) and the Phoenix branch heads up to the left. Three hundred metres from the spur the missing trestle over the B.C. Mine spur and the VV&E is encountered. A large, loose gravel abutment has to be climbed down to the spur line. This can be avoided by following the spur to the intersection. Beware: this area is littered with deep vertical mine shafts on both sides of the railway.

NOT TO SCALE

3.9   Frame trestle

This missing trestle spanned the VV&E Phoenix branch and C&W B.C. Copper Company spur. It was under this trestle that the C&W connects with the VV&E. Detour south on VV&E Phoenix branch. Just past Oro Denoro Mine take the 4x4 road 400 metres uphill to reconnect with the C&W.

The Oro Denoro Mine, km 3.5, Phoenix Subdivision.

4.1   Oro Denoro Mine spur. ⌿

4.2   Oro Denoro loading spur. ⌿

4.6   4x4 road between C&W and VV&E. ⊩←

7.9   Silica ⌿ ⅄
Phoenix Road crosses just before Silica.

8.5   Water tower. 🗼

8.8   Athelston Junction—Reffek spur ⌿ ⌿
This 5.1 kilometre-long spur line ran to B.C. Copper Company's Jackpot Mine. En route, the railway crossed one 49 metre-long frame trestle at km 1.6. The station at the mine was named Reffek after Frederic Keefer, an associate of the B.C. Copper Company. This level spur is passable and is a beautiful cycle through the forest.

9.0   Snowshoe Creek. ⋇

10.1   Water tower. 🗼

12.2   Hartford ⌿ ⅄ ⅄ ⊩⇒
A 1.5 kilometre-long spur departed here to Winnipeg Mine as the line to Phoenix switched back to head north. The spur now lies under the Lone Star Haul Road.
    The railbed from here to km 13.0 is overgrown and runs through a deep cut with some rockfall. Detour on to Lone Star Haul Road, which at km 13.0 runs atop of the original grade.

13.0   Rawhide spur. ⌿ ⊩⇐
The Lone Star Haul Road runs atop the original grade from here to Phoenix.

13.8   Snowshoe spur. ⌿

14.0   Curlew spur ⌿
Just past the open pit mine a section of one of the spurs can be found just uphill from the road.

14.3   Rawhide spur. ⌿

14.5   Snowshoe spur No. 2. ⌿

15.6   Phoenix Station. 🚋 ⌿ ⌿ ⅄

B. C. Mine Spur
4.0 kilometres

This 4.0 kilometre-long spur departs from the C&W Phoenix branch and heads east to B.C. Copper Company Mine on Thimble Mountain. The spur is a pleasant cycle through cedar forests to the mine remains at the terminus of the spur. A loading chute, donkey engine, log buildings and mine pit can be found. Thimble Mountain Trails, a 14 kilometre-long trail system maintained by the forestry department for hiking, cycling and horseback riding, departs at the end of the spur.

km

0.0   **B.C. Mine spur junction.**

0.3   C&W Phoenix branch crossed over the B.C. Mine spur and the VV&E Phoenix branch on a frame trestle. A 100 metre-long branch connected the VV&E to the C&W at this point The spur turns east toward Thimble Mountain and the branch heads straight up a slight incline to connect to the VV&E.

0.8   Highway #3
The railbed comes to an abrupt end at the ditch for Highway #3. Both sides of Highway #3 have gated fences. Across the highway the railbed is used as a logging road and is in excellent shape. There is a gate just off the highway. The railbed winds it way up through a cedar forest as it looks over Wilgress Lake.

3.5   Thimble Mountain Trail
A registration station with a map of the Thimble Mountain Trail system is found at this trailhead.

3.7   Mine buildings and a loading chute
The mine pit can be found up the hill behind the loading chute and donkey engine.

3.8   Road branches to left heading up Thimble Mountain.

4.0   **B.C. Copper Company Mine**
The wooden remains of the loading dock remain.

Log cabin by B.C. Copper Mine.

CLOSING THE CIRCLE

In following an abandoned railway, returning to your point of origin by another route is usually a lot farther and more difficult than retracing your tracks. The easiest method of return is by bus, which is available at all of the major centres on route. Cycling between these centres on the highways tends to be just as long as the railway but with grades reaching 7 to 8%. Shoulder width on these roads can vary greatly, and in the summer months, traffic can be very heavy. But for those inclined, closing the circle by bike can add a unique and alluring dimension to a cycling adventure 🚂

Here are some possibilities:

Midway to Osoyoos, 274 km (KVR)
• Return trip, 76 km on Highway #3 and pieces of VV&E.

Osoyoos to Princeton, 171.5 km (KVR)
• Return trip 113 km on Highway #3 and pieces of VV&E.

Princeton to Penticton, 113.4 km (KVR)
• Return trip 112 km on Highways #3, 3A and pieces of VV&E.

Princeton to Hope, 148.4 km (KVR)
• Return trip 133 km on Highway #3. Very hilly.

Hope to Spences Bridge, 162.8 km (KVR and NK&S)
• Return trip 142 km on Highway #1.

Grand Forks to Midway, 51 km (C&W)
• Return trip 69 km on Highway #3.

Grand Forks to Eholt, 28.2 km (C&W)
• Return trip 29.1 km on the C&W Phoenix branch to Denoro, and the VV&E Phoenix branch from Denoro.

Castlegar to Grand Forks, 111.3 km (C&W)
• Return trip 94 km on Highway #3.

NICOLA, KAMLOOPS &
SIMILKAMEEN COAL
& RAILWAY COMPANY (NK&S)
Spences Bridge to Nicola, 75.4 kilometres

This route was originally chartered in 1891 by a syndicate that included Hamilton Merritt, for whom the city of Merritt is named. The original charter was for a railway line from the CPR line at Kamloops down through Nicola to Princeton, then on to Penticton. The charter lapsed after financial backing for the railway could not be secured. In 1903 Hamilton Merritt revised the charter, adding to it the run from Spences Bridge to Nicola. By 1905, the CPR needed to access the rich coal reserves of the Nicola Valley, as they had encountered problems with their usual coal supplier on Vancouver Island. In desperation the CPR leased the charter of the NK&S from Hamilton Merritt and immediately started construction on the line in 1905. Fraught with a shortage of ties, the line was not completed until 1907. Amusingly, even once complete, the railway's poor construction had to subsequently be upgraded before it was utilized by paying traffic.

Nicola, Kamloops & Similkameen Railway
Nicola to Spences Bridge
75.4 km

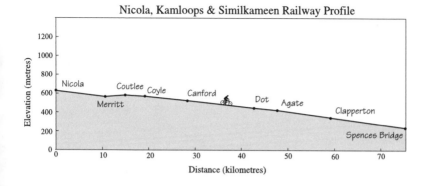

Nicola, Kamloops & Similkameen Railway Profile

This line from Spences Bridge to Nicola became known as CPR's Nicola Branch. In November of 1915, a few months following the opening of the KVR from Midway to Merritt, the CPR transferred the Nicola Branch to the KVR. With the closure of the KVR, this track was subsequently lifted in 1992, along with the remaining track south of Merritt. The B.C. government purchased the right-of-way from CPR in 1995 and the right-of-way running through the three indian reserves was returned to the reserves.

The well travelled and easy grade of this railbed entices many cyclists. Weaving through the arid Nicola Valley, the railbed crosses the Nicola River eight times. At km 60.4, the only tunnel on the Nicola branch cuts through Ten Mile Hill, and is noted for its portals made of cut stone. Along the route, the foundations and remains of most of the station houses can still be found. Many of the freight sheds are in service now as storage sheds or livestock shelters. These sheds are usually seen in the fields not far from their original locations. One interesting note is that the eight bridges that span the Nicola River along this route, are of a variety of different designs and construction.

Basically the entire length of the branch line is easily cycled, except for the section between Nicola and Merritt. The problem here is a ginseng farm which has taken over the railbed and gated the NK&S that runs through their property near Nicola and accessing the railbed between Merritt and the ginsing farm is difficult. Between Merritt and Spences Bridge the only obstructions are the many gates and gaining permission from the three indian bands to cross their reserves. Permission from each of the Indian Reserves is required to cycle the railbed through their property.

Travel connection with VIA train service, west to Vancouver or east to Jasper and Edmonton on the CNR line, can be made by taking Highway #1 to either Boston Bar, 74 kilometres south of Spences Bridge, or to Ashcroft, 43 kilometres north of Spences Bridge. An historic accommodation can be found overlooking the railway at Spences Bridge. The Steelhead Inn, which was established in 1862, has been beautifully restored with a dining room and Bed and Breakfast.

1n

Nicola, Kamloops & Similkameen Railway

km 11.2 - 31.2

An interesting side trip from Merritt is to follow along Nicola Lake to the community of Quilchena, 23 kilometres northeast of Merritt on Highway #5A. In 1907, when the line was completed to Nicola, the CPR reaffirmed its commitment to continue the line up the Nicola Valley and then down to Princeton. With this in mind, Joseph Guichon built the Quilchena Hotel in hopes of cashing in on the wealth that the passing railway would bring. Unfortunately, the railway instead headed south from Merritt down the Coldwater Valley. Today, the Quilchena Historic Hotel still operates in all its original glory, and seems to still be waiting for the railway that will never come 🚃

km   **Nicola.** ¡627 🚃 🏢 �H Υ ⚲
0.0

1.3   Ginseng Farms

     Unfortunately, the railway line appears to be lost to private interests between here and halfway to Merritt. The railbed is passable between Merritt and the other side of Ginseng Farms.

10.2   Highway #5

     The railway crosses under the highway through a culvert with no access to the highway.

11.3   Kettle Valley Railway junction. Ⅴ

11.6   **Merritt** ¡567 🚃 🏢 H Ⅴ Υ ⛺ ⛪ 🚻 🏢 (⚲

     A number of streets in Merritt cross the right-of-way giving access to the NK&S. From Merritt to Spences Bridge the railbed is in excellent shape. The dry nature of the Nicola Valley has inhibited the growth of weeds, and the sparse population of this area has fortunately created very little disruption to the railbed. The station in Merritt has been moved and can be found sitting in a field by Canford.

12.9   Nicola River—through plate girder span.)(26

14.9   **Coutlee.** ¡583 🚃 H ⚲0.1

15.1   Nicola Mameet Indian Reserve boundary—Billwiller Road ϒ

     The railbed through the Indian Reserve is private property (km 15.1–17.9). At the time of writing, no policy concerning the railbed has been resolved by the Band members. Venturing on to the reserve is at your own risk. Contact the Lower Nicola Band Administration Office for the most current status of the railbed through the reserve.

17.9   Exiting Nicola Mameet Indian Reserve.

18.0   Road. ϒ

19.2   **Coyle.** ¡570 🚃 Ⅴ ⚲0.5

19.6   Guichon Creek—half deck plate girder span.)(21

Nicola, Kamloops & Similkameen Railway
km 30.8 - 53.5

Shackan I.R.

Agate

Dot

Nooaitch

Indian

Reserve

2n

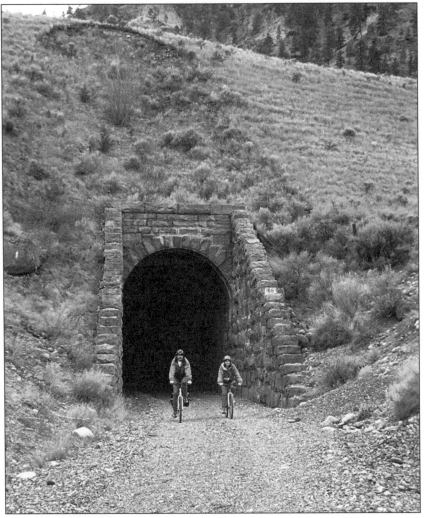

Clapperton Tunnel, km 60.0, is noted for its portals made of cut stone.

21.3   Nicola River—pony truss.)(34

23.7   Sunshine Village Road. ⊤

25.7   Graham Road. ⊤

25.9   Thornkonson Road. ⊤

26.1   Nicola River—pony truss.)(34

28.4   Canford. |525 🏠 ⫫ 🚲0.5

Nicola, Kamloops & Similkameen Railway
km 51.5 - 75.4

3n

28.6   Sunshine Village Road. ⍏

29.8   Nicola River—double through truss.)(50

29.9   Canford spur. ⍖

30.4   Petit Creek Road. ⍏

31.0   Nooaitch Indian Reserve
A gate across the railbed defines the western boundary of the reserve. The Nooaitch Indian Band has, at the time of writing, formulated no policy regarding access to the railbed. This is private property and should be respected as such. Venturing on to it is at your own risk. Contact the Nooaitch Indian Band Administration office for more information.

33.4   Water tower. ♟

41.2   Nicola River.)(50

41.7   End of Nooaitch Indian Reserve—pile trestle)(18
A gate just before the trestle defines the northern boundary of the reserve.

42.9   Dot. ⌐447 🚂 ⍖ 🚲0.5

43.8   Gordon Creek—pile trestle.)(18

45.0   Manning Creek Forestry Service Road ⍏
Gates line both sides of the road.

46.5   Nicola River—through truss.)(48

47.8   Agate. ⌐424 🚂 🚲0.8

49.1   Shackan Indian Reserve boundary—gate
The Shackan Indian Band, at the time of writing, is graciously allowing public access to the railbed through their property (km 49.1-56.1). This is private property and must be respected as such. Venturing through the reserve is at one's own risk. Contact the Shackan Band Administration for the most recent status of the trail through their property.

51.8   Water tower. ♟

52.3   Nicola River—half deck plate girder.)(50

53.5   14 Mile Ranch Road. ⍏

55.3   Highway #8 ⍏
Highway #8 has been shifted onto the original railbed for 500 metres, as both the railway and the highway are pushed against a canyon wall by the Nicola River.

For nearly the entire length of this rail line you'll cycle an excellent railbed and enjoy the dramatic scenery of the Nicola River valley.

56.1   End of Shackan Indian Reserve—gate
There are six more gates between here and Clapperton Tunnel.

59.3   Clapperton. i*348* 🏠 ⸰ 🚲*0.7*

60.0   Tunnel 🔲*99*
This 99 metre-long curved tunnel runs through Ten Mile Hill. Unique to this tunnel are the portals built of cut stone.

60.5   Highway #8. ⵔ

62.2   Highway #8. ⵔ

62.3   Nicola River—deck plate girder and deck truss.)(*50*

64.4   Water tower. 🏺

73.6   Highway #3. ⵔ

75.4   Spences Bridge i*240* 🏠 🏺 ⸰ ⎮ ⸝ ⵝ ⴷ ⌂ ‖ 🍎 ⸰ ⸰
Just prior to Spences Bridge, the NK&S parallels alongside the CPR main line. Spences Bridge shows the signs of a once more prominent railway centre. The scars of many more sidings and a wye can be seen etched into the landscape. Located at the end of the line is the historic Steelhead Inn, restaurant and hotel, established in 1862.

Some sections of the VV&E, like this tunnel at km 9.9, have been partially reclaimed by rocks or trees, but can still be explored on foot.

Vancouver, Victoria and Eastern Railway
Midway to Princeton
218.5 km

Legend:
+++++ VV&E
+++++ KVR
———— Highway
– – – Secondary Road
● Station

VANCOUVER, VICTORIA AND EASTERN RAILWAY(VV&E)
Midway to Princeton, 218.5 kilometres

The VV&E was chartered in 1896 by William Templeton, Mayor of Vancouver, as the railway to bring the riches of the Kootenays to Vancouver, a coast-to-Kootenay line. Not a spike was driven along this imaginary railway until it was taken over by J. J. Hill in 1901. As a direct competitor of the KVR, the VV&E struggled through the mountain ranges of southern B.C. and northern Washington from Midway to Brookmere. In fact, the VV&E was the first railway to reach Princeton from Midway, via Oroville, Keremeos and Hedley. It was subsequently built onward to Brookmere.

The majority of the VV&E corridor from Princeton to Oroville is not truly cyclable, but the highway follows its path closely. Some sections of the VV&E corridor between Oroville and Midway have unfortunately deteriorated past the point of being cyclable. However, there are also sections of the railway that still call out to be ridden and explored. Using the highways to bridge these sections can make for an interesting return trip, whether from Princeton to Osoyoos or Osoyoos to Midway.

Princeton to Oroville

From Princeton to the U.S. border, the VV&E generally runs beside or under the grade of Highway #3. When not under the highway, the right-of-way is in rough shape and overgrown except for a few short discontinuous sections that are in use as local access roads, thus requiring use of the highway for the most part. Both the VV&E railbed and Highway #3 pass through the towns of Hedley and Keremeos. Hedley is an old gold mining town that flourished with the help of the railway. Today, you find walking tours available of the historic sites and buildings, and you still see remnants of the workings of a mine still clinging to the mountainside. Keremeos is considered the fruit-stand capital of Canada. Back in the days of the railway, thousands of dollars worth of gold ore from the mines at Hedley passed through this town. Today, you can still find one of the original VV&E railway bridges, which is being used as a highway connection to the Ashnola River Valley, and is also the location of the favourite local swimming beach. This "Red Bridge" was built in 1907, and is one of a very few still intact.

Past Keremeos, continue along Highway #3, then branch off to Chopaka Customs to cross the U.S. border. The road continues to follow very near the VV&E. The VV&E can be accessed and is passable for 18 kilometres from Nighthawk to the outskirts of Oroville, following along the Similkameen River Valley. The arid desert valley of the Similkameen gives very little respite from a blazing sun, but the longest tunnel on the VV&E halfway to Oroville from Nighthawk will cool any cyclist by the time he gets through it. Traffic on this trail increases closer to Oroville as the citizens of this community actively use this right-of-way as a multi-use recreational trail. Oroville sits just 13 kilometres south of Osoyoos on Highway #97.

Oroville to Midway

Although it is only 76 kilometres from Osoyoos to Midway on Highway #3, there is a formidable 830 metre-high climb immediately out of Osoyoos with grades over 6%. The ultimate situation would be to connect with the VV&E at Oroville, 13 kilometres south of Osoyoos for the return trip to Midway. Unfortunately, this railbed is not totally intact and crossing the border back into Canada can create problems with customs. The only major section on the U.S. side not lost to orchards or overgrown in sagebrush is the 15 kilometres that now runs under Nine Mile Road from Circle City to Molson.

Although the distance between Oroville and Molson is only 16.9 kilometres, 37 kilometres of track was needed to assault the 850 metre elevation gain with grades near 2.4%. Circle City, about halfway between Oroville and Molson, was named after the large loop that was needed to gain the elevation required to get to Molson. This loop is now a large scar in a farmer's field. Along Nine Mile Road there are many plaques in memory of the railway and the towns that the VV&E affected.

At the near ghost town of Molson, the evidence of the VV&E is still clearly visible. The broad expanse of land for the many sidings, the wye and the station foundation are clearly evident in the middle of town. Located at the southern corner of Molson is an outdoor museum with many preserved and restored buildings of an earlier period of time. To get to Circle City from Oroville, take the Oroville/Cheesaw Road to Nine Mile Road. At the Nine Mile Road intersection, the VV&E grade crosses the Oroville/Cheesaw Road twice as it makes a lazy loop up the side of the hill. You will notice that the trestles are missing, as with most of the trestles on the VV&E.

On the Canadian side of the border two sections of the VV&E invite exploration. The first from Bridesville to Myncaster can be incorporated into the return loop from Osoyoos to Midway. At Bridesville, the railway

218

grade is clearly visible as it switchbacks up and around the town and crosses Highway #3. For a short distance the highway follows on top of the original grade running right past the original station site. To get on the VV&E take the gravel road heading south out of Bridesville. This road crosses the railway in less than a kilometre. From this point the right-of-way is generally passable, although some bushwhacking and minor detours are required around missing trestles and one tunnel on the way to Myncaster.

At Myncaster there was a station, water tank, customs house and post office. A large horseshoe trestle spanned the valley with its apex mere metres from the Canada-U.S. border. On the west side of the trestle a spur line headed south across the border to Bolster, Washington. The horseshoe trestle and tracks were removed in 1936. Those trestles that barely remain standing are no longer safe to cross.

From Myncaster the railway becomes more difficult to follow. Between Myncaster and Midway the VV&E passed through four tunnels and numerous trestles. Few of the trestles remain standing and a couple of the tunnel entrances are virtually blocked by rock slides. Compounding this, segments of the right-of-way have been reclaimed by the vegetation. Poor access and lack of detours around obstacles makes it almost impossible to continue from Myncaster to Midway. This is unfortunate as this is one of the most beautiful sections of the VV&E as it follows along the Myers Creek Valley. Myncaster Road reconnects with Highway #3 at Rock Creek.

The other section that can be followed is from Midway to the 260 metre-long tunnel, at km 9.9. The Midway Dump Road now runs atop the original VV&E grade for 9.1 kilometres. At km 5.0 is the disputed parcel of land that resulted in the Battle of Midway. Departing from the road at km 9.1 the tunnel can be found 0.7 kilometres farther down the VV&E grade. Leave your bikes at the entrance because at the other end, the right-of-way is so overgrown with trees that even travel on foot is difficult. Be careful, the tunnel is curved and dark. Halfway through the tunnel the ties are still in place and tripping over them is common. One kilometre of bushwhacking past the tunnel, the missing trestle over Myers Creek makes further travel impossible ▰

km   **Midway** ▰ ♦ ♪ ⋏ ♨ ⼝ ♦

0.0   The railbed is passable from Midway to the tunnel at km 9.9, following the Midway Dump Road for the most part.

6.5   Hooligan siding ♪
          Named for the "Battle of Midway," which occurred here when the VV&E drove tracks across a piece of property owned by the CPR.

9.9   Tunnel ▰274
          Past the tunnel, the railbed is impassable to bicycles but can be hiked to km 11.5.

10.3 Roberts spur. ▰ ♪

Molson, km 49.3, was a thriving railway centre in the early 1900s. Today, the memories live on in the "Ye Old Molson" outdoor museum.

Easy cycling and peaceful surroundings make this section between Bridesville and Myncaster a perfect destination for a lazy afternoon, approximately km 34.0.

11.5   Myers Creek ✝181

Although the railbed is passable after Myers Creek, there is no way to bypass this missing bridge.

13.6   Bergen. 🏠 🚻 ⑂

15.0   Tunnel ◼35

Frequently used by horse campers.

15.2   Myers Creek ✝ ✝151

The valley can be crossed utilizing small bridges placed across the many faceted streams of Myers Creek. A 4x4 access road from Rock Creek intersects the railway.

16.8   Tunnel. ◼34

21.1   Bridge)(55

Still standing but not for long. It is not advisable to cross on this bridge.

21.8   Myers Creek—horseshoe trestle ✝249x27

The apex of this huge trestle came within six metres of the international border. Only the fill approaches remain. Myncaster Road crosses underneath the west approach.

22.2   Myncaster spur ⑂

This spur line heads south across the border for a couple of hundred metres. It was intended to run to Cheesaw about eight kilometres south of here.

22.7   Myncaster 🏠 🚻 ⑂

Although somewhat overgrown in spots, the railbed is cyclable for the majority of the distance from Myncaster to Bridesville.

25.0   Tunnel ◼107

The entrances of this tunnel are almost covered by rock slides. A road bypasses the tunnel to the east.

28.1   Rock Mountain Forest Service Road ✝

The VV&E crosses a paved road from Rock Creek. From this intersection the railbed is utilized as a forest service road.

30.6   Syackan. 🏠 ⑂

35.1   Dumont. ⑂

35.5   McCoy Creek ✝ ✝

The VV&E crossed over McCoy Creek Road and McCoy Creek on this missing trestle.

37.9   Bridesville Road ☨

Past this road, travel on the railway becomes discontinuous and troublesome.

41.3   Bridesville 🏠 ⛪

The VV&E loops up and around this small community. For a short section the railbed is under Highway #3 as it passes by the town. Past Bridesville, the VV&E crosses though farmland and is plowed under in spots, overgrown in others and not generally passable.

46.2   International border.

49.3   Molson 🏠 ⛪ ♙ ⸜ ⮌

Molson was a major railway centre, sporting numerous sidings, spurs and a wye. Today the scars on the landscape around Molson still tell the story of those early days when the railway was an important part of this community. Heading north out of Molson, Nine Mile Road runs atop the original railbed until the Oroville/Cheesaw Road intersection.

57.3   Porters. 🏠

60.7   Ninemile 🏠

The railway follows the first of many loops as it starts its descent to Oroville. The road departs the railbed briefly as the VV&E carves out a couple of large loops as it descends the hillside. At the bottom of the loops the two reconnect.

67.3   Circle City 🏠

Past Circle City, Nine Mile Road departs from the VV&E and connects to the Oroville/Cheesaw Road. The railbed continues as a rough overgrown scar in the arid landscape. Cycling is not possible past this point. There are a couple of discontinuous sections between here and Oroville that can be cycled, but accessing them is difficult.

78.4   Mount Hull. 🏠

84.2   Oroville/Cheesaw Road. ☨

86.3   Great Northern junction. ⸜ Y

87.7   Oroville 🏠 ⛪ ♙ ⛺ 🏛 ⛩ ⛏ ☾

From Oroville to Nighthawk the railbed is being used as a multi-use trail.

95.7   Tunnel. ▮

105.9 Nighthawk 🏠

Past Nighthawk, it soon becomes impossible to cycle the railbed.

114.5 Ruby Mines. 🏠

This "Red Bridge" in Keremeos dates back to 1907 and the days when the Great Northern Railway dominated this area.

124.1 Chopaka. 🏠 ⸶

124.2 International border

From the international border to Cawston, the VV&E spends the majority of its length within the boundaries of three Indian reservations. Owing to the number of bridges missing, and the lack of traffic on this section, there are no notable segments that can be cycled.

126.8 Sneuhumption Creek. ⭤ *34*

128.4 Delmar. 🏠

130.8 Similkameen River. ⭤ *185*

132.6 Bridge. ⭤ *36*

133.6 Similkameen River. ⭤ *63*

133.7 Similkameen River. ⭤ *257x11*

134.4 Bridge. ⭤ *51*

139.7 Similkameen. 🏠 ⸶

145.0 Cawston 🏠 ⸶ ⸙ (

From Cawston to Keremeos the railbed follows alongside the highway; it is in rough shape and overgrown.

147.7 Spur. ⌇

151.6 Keremeos. 🚌 🏕️ 🍴 △ ♨ ⛺ 🚻

155.9 Similkameen River)(287

This through timber truss-covered bridge is still in use today as the Ashnola Road Bridge. The Ashnola Road is built upon the original grade until km 161.3. From km 161.3 to the missing bridge over the Ashnola River, the grade is marginally passable but is within the Asnola Indian Reserve.

162.1 Ashnola River. ✝70

162.2 Ashnola. 🚌

167.1 Similkameen River. ✝208

172.4 Bradshaw 🚌

Past Bradshaw, sections of this right-of-way are in marginally cyclable condition, though accessing the railbed can be a problem. There are a few roads that cross the railbed; the railbed does touch the highway in a couple of places.

173.6 Highway #3. ⛳

179.6 Highway #3. ⛳

179.8 Hedley. 🚌 🏕️ 🍴 ⌇ △ ♨ ⛺ 🚻

180.1 Hedley Creek. ✝239

181.9 Similkameen River. ✝280

186.2 Henri Creek. ✝44

186.8 Highway #3 ⛳

Just before Cory, Highway #3 crosses the Similkameen River and turns on to the VV&E right-of-way, following it to Princeton. At this junction, the VV&E can be followed back to the missing bridge over the Similkameen River at km 181.9. This section of the right-of-way is in good shape and is used as a local road.

188.1 Cory. 🚌 ⌇

189.1 Smith Creek. ✝34

198.9 Bromley. 🚌 🍴

201.6 Wolf Creek. ✝42

204.4   Spring Creek. ⵝ 26

206.6 Norman. 🚃 ⌇

210.0   Short spur. ⌇

214.2 Allison. 🚃

215.2   Portland Cement Plant spur ⌇
 This spur runs 2.6 kilometres to the Portland Cement Plant. Past the cement plant the spur crosses the KVR Princeton Subdivision at km 109.2. Because it was abandoned so many years ago, it is difficult to find.

217.4   Spur. ⌇

217.6   Similkameen River. ⵝ

217.7   Kettle Valley Railway junction. ⌇

218.5 Princeton. 🚃 ⬧ ⌇ ⌇ ⵙ 🏛 🚉 ⬧ (

Laying track on the KVR into Princeton in 1915. VV&E bridge into Princeton can be seen in the background. (Princeton Museum)

Future Development

Following the abandonment of the Kettle Valley Railway, a corridor remained that had incredible potential for development into a long distance, multi-use trail. There is strong public sentiment in B.C. for garnering abandoned rail lines as public assets. With this in mind, the British Columbia government voiced strong commitment to preserve the KVR corridor so that it can play a part in the future of British Columbia just as it did in its past. It is recognized that the KVR right-of-way is of most value as an intact, publicly owned corridor, held and managed by the province. Over many years, and with the coordinated efforts of numerous groups and individuals, the conversion of the abandoned Kettle Valley Railway to a multi-use corridor is beginning to be realized.

Some of the key issues concerning the rail-to-trail conversion of the KVR:

• Lack of continuous ownership of the right-of-way. The B.C. government is presently negotiating for ownership of as much of the complete corridor as possible.

• Concerns voiced by adjacent landowners who are fearful of vandalism or who object that the right-of-way bisects their property.

• Differing recreational or industrial uses. Planning is required to determine which combination of industrial and recreational uses should occur on various sections of the right-of-way, and at which times of the season.

• Protection of sensitive natural environments. There is concern that increased public access to sensitive ecosystems, such as the bird sanctuary at Vaseux Lake, may disrupt this unusual and fragile site.

• Funding for trail conversion and maintenance. It has been voiced that funding should come from a combined effort of government, corporations using the right-of-way, and contributions of community groups and recreationists using the trail.

• Preserving and heightening awareness of heritage values. Many significant structures need protection from the threat of vandalism or natural degradation. Regional interpretive centres, community events and information plaques along the rail-trail routes can all be used to heighten awareness of heritage resources.

The Carmi Subdivision has seen much progress over the last few years toward achieving a multi-use trail. The KVR right-of-way from Midway to Penticton was acquired by the province of British Columbia in 1990. The KVR Corridor Project was initiated in 1991 by the Ministry of Forests, through the Penticton Forest District. An integrated resource management plan was completed in 1993, with recommendations for future use and management of the KVR right-of-way from Midway to Glenfir. To achieve acceptable standards for a designated multi-use trail, repairs to tunnels, trestles, bridges and right-of-way upgrading is required. Some areas will need roads and/or new access routes as well as cattle guards, fences and barriers. Some areas may also require rerouting to maintain a continuous corridor. Over the next few years, implementation of these plans will result in the completion of this KVR multi-use corridor.

In conjunction with various government agencies, many societies and organized groups are also playing a large hand in coordinating the management of the rail-to-trail corridor of the Carmi Subdivision. For example, B.C. Parks is one of the agencies responsible for Myra Canyon; however, the Myra Canyon Trestle Restoration Society is a volunteer group that has coordinated much of the funding, materials, services and manpower in upgrading the 18 Myra Canyon trestles to acceptable park standards. The coordinated efforts of the city of Penticton, the Greenbelt Preservation Society and the Penticton Rotary Club have also enabled the preservation and upgrading of the KVR corridor through the city limits of Penticton.

The Osoyoos Subdivision's right-of-way, from Okanagan Falls to Osoyoos, was acquired by the province of British Columbia in 1990. The International Bicycling and Hiking Society has played a key role in establishing 17.4 kilometres of this trail along the Okanagan River Channel, ending at the north end of Okanagan Lake. At present, there is no planned development from the end of this trail to Osoyoos. However, development north of this trail to Okanagan Falls remains in the planning stages. The main concern is the fragile ecosystem of Vaseux Lake. One of the proposed solutions is to reroute the trail to the east side of the lake, which already accommodates a lot of traffic. The remaining section along Skaha Lake is still being negotiated. Since much of this section is within the Penticton Indian Reserve, the rail-trail planning is having to explore various alternatives.

The right-of-way of the Princeton Subdivision has now been acquired by the province of British Columbia. Unfortunately, with time vandalism found its way to some of the historic landmarks and trestles. Now that ownership of the land is secured, progress will hopefully move forward much in the same way as that of the Carmi Subdivision. Some of the active groups along the Princeton Subdivision are the Rails-to-Trails Society, the Okanagan-Similkameen Parks Society, the Outdoor Recreation Council of B.C. and the Kettle Valley Railway (KVR) Heritage Society. One unique feature of the KVR Heritage Society is that they have not only preserved the corridor, but they are presently running a heritage railway from Winslow to Faulder with plans to reconstruct the stations in the theme of the 1930s. This brings an incomparably unique feature to this subdivision.

Acquiring the right-of-way of the Merritt Subdivision occurred in 1995, along with the section of railbed that follows north from Merritt to Spences Bridge (CPR's Nicola branch). Some sections bisect Indian Reservation Land, which will require subsequent negotiations to use this corridor or possible rerouting of the trail. The Rails-to-Trails Society and the Outdoor Recreation Council of B.C. are some of the groups that have a forefront involvement with the development of these subdivisions.

The Coquihalla Subdivision is unique in that much of the right-of-way has already been put to alternative use. The entire subdivision is provincially owned, with some sections now lying under the grade of the Coquihalla Highway and other sections incorporated into the grade of the Transmountain Pipeline Road. However, more importantly are the many areas that have been designated recreation areas with information plaques regarding the Kettle Valley Railway, such as those found at Juliet and Othello. It is unlikely that the near future will bring any significant change to the Coquihalla Subdivision. Unfortunately, Mother Nature has not been so kind to the railway. In 1996, severe spring flooding caused pieces of the trail to literally be washed into the canyon, making it very difficult to follow this trail and necessitating detours. However, this corridor in conjunction with the Carmi and Princeton subdivisions may form a key component for a trans-provincial trail, as no other options exist along this general route. These rail-trails would thus form a key component for Canada's National Trail, which is currently being developed.

It seems that all involved unanimously agree that the Kettle Valley Railway corridor is a valuable resource with great recreational, historical and environmental potential. Maintaining this unique corridor enables us to get in touch with the land, the people and the history of British Columbia ▅▅

The Kettle Valley Railway Heritage Society is working to preserve the last 16 kilometres of the KVR and an important part of Canadian history. A working steam railway museum, operating in the style of the 1930s, will be established from Winslow to Faulder. The train itself is now pumping steam and taking passengers.

Groups Involved with Rail-Trail Conversion

Outdoor Recreation Council of B.C.
334-1367 West Broadway
Vancouver, B.C. V6H 4A9
Phone: (604) 737-3058
Fax: (604) 737-3666
email:
outrec_council@pop.mindlink.net

Boundary Rails-to-Trails Society
c/o Chris Moslin
Grand Forks, B.C.
Phone: (250) 442-2620
email: crmoslin@mail.awinc.com

**Okanagan-Similkameen
Parks Society**
c/o Sheila White
Box 787, Summerland, B.C.
V0H 1Z0
Phone: (250) 494-8996
Fax: (250) 494-1415

**International Bicycling
& Hiking Society**
c/o John Bremmer
Box 5, Oliver, B.C. V0H 1T0
Phone: (250) 498-4781
Fax: (250) 498-4781

**Princeton-Brookmere
Rails-to-Trails Society**
c/o Johanna Poier-Nott
PO 1926, Princeton, B.C.
Phone: (250) 295-3875

Kettle Valley Steam Railway
Phone: (250) 494-8422
Fax: (250) 494-8452
Open mid-May to mid-October

**Kettle Valley Railway
Heritage Society**
c/o Ken Tapping
Phone: (250) 492-6370

Trans Canada Trail Corporation
6104 Sherbrooke West
Montreal, PQ H4A 1Y3
Phone: 1-800-465-3636

**Myra Canyon Trestle
Restoration Society**
c/o Tibor Balogh
1046 Wilson Ave.
Kelowna, B.C.
V1Y 6Y3
Phone: (250) 860-6261

Nicola Rails-to-Trails Society
c/o Jennifer Trudeau
RR1, S21, C9, Merritt, B.C.

Kettle Valley Corridor Project
Ministry of Forests
Penticton Forest District
c/o Barbara Pryce
102 Industrial Place
Penticton, B.C.
V2A 7C8
Phone: (250) 490-2200
Fax: (250) 492-1283

B.C. Ministry of Parks
Southern Interior Regional Office
101 - 1050 West Columbia Street
Kamloops, B.C. V2C 1L4
Phone: (250) 828-4501

B.C. Ministry of Forests
c/o Kamloops Regional Office
515 Columbia Street
Kamloops, B.C. V2C 2T7
Phone: (250) 828-4137

**Canadian Rails
to Greenways Network**
c/o Ann Robinson
5430 Riverside Crescent
Manotick, ON K4M 1G9
Phone: (613) 692-3934

**The Slocan Valley Heritage
Trail Society**
Box 76, Winlaw, B.C. V0G 2J0
Phone: (250) 226-7849

Accommodations

There are many accommodations available along the KVR route. Picnicking, camping and lodging facilities are all conveniently located. The following list is not meant to be a recommendation of any particular facility, but to provide a guide to those facilities that are on or readily accessed from the KVR right-of-way. We have not listed the numerous facilities that are available in the larger centres such as Penticton. We recommend obtaining a B.C. Accommodation Guide, available from B.C. Travel Infocentres or Tourism British Columbia, Legislature Buildings, Victoria, B.C. V8V 1X4
1-800-663-6000 / (604) 387-1642

If phoning any facility in British Columbia, note that the area code is now 250, except for the lower mainland, which is 604, i.e. Vancouver and Hope.

Carmi Subdivision
(Midway to Penticton)

Midway Motor Inn (km 0.0)
622 Palmerston Street, Box 330, Midway V0H 1M0. Air conditioned, satellite cable TV, licensed dining, 449-2662.

Kettle River Inn & Saloon (km 0.0)
Located across from Kettle River and community campground in Midway. Originally the old Thomet Hotel built in 1900, licensed dining, 449-2288.

Frank Carpenter Memorial Park (km 0.0)
Located on Kettle River in Midway—Florence Street and 5th Avenue. Community campground, washrooms, no showers, 449-2222.

Jim Blaine Campground (km 16.1)
Community campground, sports and picnic area, flush toilets, water, picnic tables.

The Rock Creek Hotel & Prospector Pub (km 18.8)
Junction Highway #3 & #33 in Rock Creek. Cozy bedrooms, garden patio overlooking Kettle River, fine pub food in the ambiance of the oldest continuous operating pub in B.C., 446-2474.

Edelweiss Inn & Motel (km 18.8)
Highway #3, Rock Creek, 10 sleeping units, licensed restaurant, 446-2400.

Kettle River Recreation Area (km 25.2)
Campground situated in a ponderosa pine forest, flush toilets, showers, water, picnic tables, pay phone.

Beaverdell Campground (km 68.1)
Community campground next to bridge crossing Kettle Valley River in the open grassy area next to river, pit toilets.

Beaverdell Hotel (km 68.1)
Highway #33, Beaverdell, 484-5513. Oldest operating heritage hotel in British Columbia, sleeping units, shared baths, dining and pub.

Tamarack Lodge (km 68.1)
Highway #33, Beaverdell, 484-5616. Sleeping units, shared bath, dining area.

Arlington Lakes Campground (km 98.2)
Primitive but scenic campsite in the trees on the southwest shore of the southernmost Arlington Lake. Pit toilets, picnic tables.

Summit Lake Campground (km 119)
Open-treed campground on shore of Hydraulic Lake. Pit toilets, water, picnic tables, used as staging area for horseback riding.

Idabel Lake Resort (turn off at km 117.1)
Idabel Lake, c/o RR#5, Site 13E, Comp 2, Kelowna V1X 4K4. Well-developed cottages (linen not

supplied) and campground overlooking Idabel Lake, 4.2 kilometres
from KVR. Laundry, showers,
licensed restaurant/coffee shop,
store, playground, 762-1421.

Summit Lake Campsite (km 119.7)
Ministry of Forests campsite, pit
toilets, picnic tables.

Hydraulic Lake Campsite (km 120.8)
Ministry of Forests campsite, pit
toilets, picnic tables.

McCulloch Lake Resort and Campground (km 121.2)
Hydraulic Lake, c/o Site 13C, Apt. 8,
RR5, Kelowna C1X 4K4. Overlooking
Hydraulic Lake, cabins with wood
stoves (linen not supplied), campground, showers, flush toilets, more
facilities in plans for 1997. Phone
Nancy or Jim Pollard: 491-8804 or
862-7834.

Chute Lake Resort (km 171.4)
Chute Lake, c/o RR#1, Site 16, Comp 16,
Naramata V0H 1N0.
Large lodge in antique decor with
sleeping rooms overlooking Chute
Lake, rustic log cabins (linen extra)
and campground, showers, flush
toilets, laundry, licensed restaurant/
coffee shop, meals may be ordered
from the regular menu, dinner is by
reservation, 493-3535.

Naramata (turn off at km 200.3)
Naramata Canyon on the Falls B & B,
1490 Smethurst Place, 496-5321.
Two rooms: two-acre setting with
view of lake and waterfall, private
baths and outdoor hot tub. Kettle
Valley Railway km 200 is 1/3 km
away.

Ringabella B & B, 2486 Gammon Rd,
Naramata, 496-4184.
One room: log home opposite Lang
Winery.

Scotch Corner B & B, 950 Tillar Rd.,
Naramata, 496-4290.
Two rooms: hearty breakfast, hot tub.

Paradise Cove B & B, 3129 Hayman Rd.,
Naramata, 496-5896.
Three rooms: panoramic lake view,
private baths, phones, hot tub.

Penticton (km 215.0)
Numerous camping and lodging
accommodations.

The Brough House B & B, 185 Middle
Bench Rd. S., Penticton, 490-9958.
Three rooms: 1916 character home,
indoor pool.

Riordan House B & B, 689 Winnipeg St.,
Penticton, 493-5997.
Three rooms: 1921 heritage home,
antique decor, fireplace.

Eagle's Point B & B, 3145 Juniper Drive,
Penticton, 493-6555.
Four rooms: lookalike castle on
mountain with view of city below.

Castle Rock B & B, 2050 Sutherland Road,
Penticton, 492-4429.
Three rooms: log home with pool
close to KVR trail km 206.9.

Apex Mountain Ranch, Main Stn.,
Penticton, 492-2454. Three rooms.

Budget B & B, 230 Farrell St., Penticton,
492-6743. Three rooms.

Memory Inn B & B, 2510 Dartmouth Dr.,
Penticton, 493-9368. Three rooms.

Slinn's Place, 29000 Valleyview Rd.,
Penticton, 492-8176. Two rooms.

Susan's Place, 161 Huth Ave., Penticton,
493-2167. Two rooms.

God's Mountain Crest Chalet, Eastside
Lake Rd., Penticton 490-4800.
Four rooms, seven cabins: located on
six acre vineyard within 100 acre
mountain park.

Osoyoos Subdivision
(Penticton to Osoyoos)

Banbury Green RV Park (km 8.4)
Pine Drive, Box 237, Penticton, V2A 6X3.
Tents welcome, showers, phone,
laundry, flush toilets, 497-5221.

Ponderosa Point Resort (km 12)
319 Ponderosa Avenue, Box 106, Kaleden,
V0H 1K0, 497-5354.
Fully-equipped one and three
bedroom cottages with view of Skaha
Lake. Cable TV, phone, playground,
tennis court, 25 units.

Sage Pine B&B, 153 Cedar Ave., Kaleden,
497-6382.
Two rooms: pool lake view, private
entrance and bath.

Smith & Wife B&B, 230 Ponderosa Ave.,
Kaleden 497-5536.
Two rooms: lake view, private bath,
adjacent to beach and trail.

Okanagan Falls (km 17.1)

Numerous camping and lodging
accommodations.

**Willow House B & B, 1136 Willow Street,
OK Falls, 497-5148.**
Three rooms: private entrance, guest
living room with fridge and TV.

Grey Sage B&B, Highway #97, OK Falls,
497-8138, one room and teepee.

Vaseux Lake Provincial Park
(Highway #97 detour route).
Highway #97, four kilometres south
of Okanagan Falls.
Camping, swimming, water, toilets,
494-0321.

Vaseux Lake Campground
(Highway #97 detour route).
Highway #97 North, RR#2, Vaseux
Lake, Oliver, V0H 1T0.
Orchard setting, toilets, showers,
sandy beach, 40 sites, 498-4234.

Oliver (km 36.5)

Numerous camping and lodging
accommodations.

Fritzville B&B, 34032 Highway #97 St.,
Oliver, 498-3645.
One room: private entrance/bath-
room, full kitchenette, pool, orchard
setting.

AnneMarie's B&B, 34427-97 St., Oliver,
498-0131. Two rooms: private baths.

Orchard Ridge Guest House, 12346-318th
Ave., Oliver, 498-4786.
Three rooms: panoramic view of
valley, large garden and pool.

The Log House B&B, 30864 Highway #97,
Oliver, 498-0414.
Three rooms: Danish/German hospital-
ity in the heart of wine and fruit
country.

Mirror Lake Guesthouse, 9551-306 Ave. and
Highway #97, Oliver, 495-7959.
Three rooms: heritage farmhouse,
private lake, midway between Oliver
and Osoyoos.

Wildflower B&B, Oliver, 498-4326. Two
rooms: outdoor activities.

Osoyoos (km 58.1)

Numerous camping and lodging
accommodations.

Haynes Point Lakeside Guesthouse, 3619
Jasmine Drive, Osoyoos, 495-7443.
Three rooms: modern hillside
rancher overlooking Prov. Park.

Lake Osoyoos Guesthouse, 5809 Oleander
Drive, Osoyoos, 495-3297.
Three rooms: self-contained suites,
beachfront with dock, BBQ.

Reflections Guest House, 6813
Meadowlark Drive, Osoyoos, 495-5229.

Princeton Subdivision (Penticton to Brookmere)
Summerland (km 15.3)

Nine camping/lodging accommodations.

Laur-o-win House B&B, 16423 Kean St., Summerland, 494-1973. Three rooms.

Okanagan Lakeview B&B, 11591 Front Bench Rd., Summerland, 494-9856. One suite: self-contained suite with separate entrance.

Lakeshore Memories B&B, 12216 Lakeshore Dr., Summerland, 494-5134. Three rooms: restored heritage home by lake and restaurants.

Heidi's B&B, Giants Head Rd., Summerland, 494-0833. Three rooms: Llama hobby farm near the "Kettle Valley Steam Railway" Summerland Station.

Lake Inn B&B, 7219 Nixon Rd., Summerland, 494-1825. Three rooms: on the beach, hot tub, menu, guest living room.

Lakeview B&B, Summerland, 494-8556. Three rooms, view and hot tub.

Alice Road Inn, 16109 Alice Rd., Summerland, 494-8158. Two rooms.

F&F B&B, 12514 Barnes St., Summerland, 494-1993. Five rooms.

Heritage House B&B, 11919 Jubilee Rd., Summerland, 494-0039. Three rooms.

Twisty Hazel B&B, 13808 Spencer Ave., Summerland, 494-3175. Three rooms.

Thirsk Lake Campsite (km 55)
Ministry of Forests campsite on the shore of Thirsk Lake.

Chain Lake Campsite (km 71.1)
Ministry of Forests campsite on the shore of Chain Lake.

Princeton Castle Campground/RV Park (km 109.9)
Highway #40, Box 2050, Princeton V0X 1W0, 295-6250. Overlooking Allison Creek, restaurant, hiking trails, tours of the Portland Cement Plant historic ruins, showers, laundry.

Woodside Inn B&B
141 W. China Creek Road, Princeton, 295-3554, 1-800-880-0822. Four rooms: pool, hot tub, acreage setting.

Coalmont Hotel (km 132.3)
Built in 1912, newly restored with antique decor. Five sleeping units, shared baths, public dining area, pub, 295-6066.

Granite Creek (km 132.3)
At the junction of Tulameen River and Granite Creek. Ministry of Forests campsite located at the original site of Granite City.

Otter Sleep Inn (km 138.7)
Otter Avenue, c/o Box 2B, Comp 7, Tulameen, 295-7494. Six units: combination baths, pay phone, near laundry and the Tulameen Trading Post store and restaurant.

Otter Lake Provincial Park (km 139.1)
Large park on the shores of Otter Lake. Camping, picnic sites, water, pit toilets, swimming, fishing.

Kershar Horse Motel (km 168.5)
c/o Kershar, Smiles, N. Otter Valley Road, Box 2A, Comp 2, Tulameen. A rustic vacation spot for you and your horse (or bike), tenting only, pit toilets, no showers. Contact person Burt Sharkey.

Merritt / Nicola Subdivision (Brookmere to Merritt / Nicola to Spences Bridge)

Quilchena Hotel,
Box 1, Quilchena, 378-2611.
Sixteen units: located on Nicola Lake, 1908 heritage hotel, dining and pub, golf, swimming, horseback trips, boat and bike rentals.

Merritt (km 47.3 Merritt Sub / km 11.6 Nicola Sub)

Numerous camping and lodging accommodations.

A.P. Guest Ranch, Highway #5A—Merritt-Princeton Highway, 378-6520.

Winding River Guest Ranch, Torgerson Rd., Merritt, 378-6534. Three cabins.

Guichon Creek Outdoor Adventures, 322 Guichon Ave., Lower Nicola.
Near "KVR's" Nicola Subdivision, 378-2065.
Two rooms and cabin: day kitchen, hot tub, bike rentals, guided tours.

Grant Ranches Ltd., Aberdeen Rd., Lower Nicola, 378-9865. Two rooms.

Aberdeen Inn & Pub, 318 Aberdeen, Lower Nicola, Merritt, 378-2868.

Steelhead Inn (km 75.4—Nicola Sub)
Box 100, Spences Bridge, V0K 2L0, 458-2398.
Fourteen units: 1862 historic hotel located at the end of the Nicola line. Full breakfast included, licensed dining, riverside patio, river rafting.

Quarter Circle J Motel, Riverview Avenue, Spences Bridge, 458-2223.
Seventeen units: fishing, dining, general store, river rafting, hiking.

Spences Bridge

Motels, campgrounds and the local pub are all located in the town on the north side of the Thompson River.

Coquihalla Subdivision (Brookmere to Hope)

Coquihalla Lakes Lodge and Campsite (km 28.9)
Located on 1/3 mile lakefront on Coquihalla Lakes.
Large, medium or honeymoon cabins, camping, fishing, boat and equipment rentals, (250) 378-0038.

Othello Tunnels Campground (km 78.7)
67851 Othello Road, Box 2009, Hope, V0X 1L0.
Walking distance from the tunnels. Flush toilets, laundry, showers, pay phone, store, 30 sites, (604) 869-9448.

Coquihalla Campsite (km 85.7)
800 Kawkawa Lake Road, Hope, V0X 1L0.
Camping along the Coquihalla River. Showers, laundry, firepits, covered barbecue area, recreation/playground area, convenience store, 130 sites, (604) 869-7119.

Hope (km 87.4)

Numerous camping and lodging accommodations.

Simon's on Fraser B&B,
Hope, (604) 869-2562.

Columbia & Western Railway (Castlegar to Midway)

Castlegar (km 0.0)

Numerous camping and hotel accommodations.

Mountain Retreat Guest House,
Castlegar, 365-9396.

Robson Homestead B&B, 3671 Broadwater Rd., Castlegar, 365-2374.
Two rooms: 1909 restored home on three acres, antique furnished rooms.

Blue Berry Hill B&B, 145 Fairview Dr., Castlegar, 365-5583.
Two rooms: cozy country home, homegrown fruit preserves.

The Greenhouse B&B, Syringa Creek Park, Castlegar, 365-2696. Two rooms.

Chistina Lake (exit C&W from Fife km 82.2)

Numerous lodging accomodations in Christina Lake.

Royal Inn B&B, 1 Chase Rd., Christina Lake, 447-9090.
One room: private entrance, view of lake, near public beach on south end of lake, exit C&W on Santa Rosa, then turn south on highway turning on West Lake Rd.

Ruby's Garden B&B, 94 Holmes Rd., Christina Lake, 447-6693.
Two rooms: near public beach on south end of lake, exit C&W on Santa Rosa.

Cascade Cove Campground (km 90.1)
1290 River Road, Christina Lake, junction of Highway #3 & U.S. 395; turn north off C&W at intersection with U.S. 395, ph. 447-6163.
Sixty sites: on Kettle River, quiet, off highway, tenting, free showers, playground, sandy beach, swimming.

Country Hideaway RV Park & Campground (exit C&W from km 105.4)
Manly Meadows Road, ph. 442-2341, five kilometres east off Highway #3, turn south at Whitehall Road (km 105.4) then follow signs. Twenty-seven sites located on the Kettle River, flush toilets, showers, swimming, sandy beach.

Riviera RV Park & Campground, Highway #3—two kilometres east of Grand Forks, 442-2158.
Thirty-three sites: pay phone, flush toilets, hot showers, shady area on the Kettle River.

Grand Forks (km 111.3)

Numerous lodging accommodations in town.

Grand Forks Municipal Park & Campground, 442-2833.
Located two blocks south of Highway #3 on 5th Street. Twenty-eight sites: flush toilets, showers, firepits, river swimming, near downtown shopping area, sandy beach and playground.

The White House B&B, 1350-73 Ave., Grand Forks, 442-8481.
Two rooms: country charm in turn-of-the-century home, near downtown.

The Powell House B&B, 981 Central Ave., Grand Forks, 442-5737.
Two rooms: antique decor in heritage home, near downtown.

The Dewdney Trail B&B, 3555 Sion Frontage Road, Grand Forks, 442-5757.
Three rooms: spacious modern home, sitting room with wood stove.

The Orchard B&B, 5615 Spencer Rd., Grand Forks, 442-8583.
Two rooms: nestled in an orchard overlooking Sunshine Valley, laundry avail.

Greenwood (km 147.8)

Greenwood Motel & Campground, 256 North Copper St., 445-6363.
Twelve units: flush toilets, showers, pay phone, close to downtown.

Evening Star Motel, 798 North Government St., Greenwood, 445-6733.
Eleven units: air conditioned, large family units, D.D. phone, satellite TV, store.

The Forshow House B&B, 197 Kimberly Ave. S., Greenwood, 445-2208.
Three rooms: restored heritage house, great breakfast, non-smoking.

Boundary Creek Provincial Park (km 152.0)
Eighteen sites: camping, pit toilets, located on the east side of Boundary Creek. The creek is easily forded at the campsite or you can exit the railway at km 154.1 on Boltz Road, then continue along the highway to the campground, 825-4421.

Boundary Falls Ranch and Campground, 445-6578.
Forty sites: Eight kilometres west of Greenwood on Highway #3.

Midway (km 162.3)

For accommodations refer to the KVR Carmi Subdivision (Midway to Penticton).

Tour Operators

Frontier Travel

Supported camping and lodge-to-lodge trips.
(604) 730-1247
Fax (604) 738-7655
rem@mindlink.bc.ca

R.E.M. Event Management

Yearly supported bike trip on the KVR.
(604) 878-8000
Fax (604) 738-7655
rem@mindlink.bc.ca

Monashee Mountain Bike Tours

1591 Highland Dr., North Kelowna, V1Y 4K6
(250) 762-9253

Company of Adventurers

Guichon Creek Outdoor Adventures Bike rentals and guided tours.
322 Guichon Avenue, Lower Nicola
(250) 378-2065

Okanagan Bicycle Tours

11059 Eva Road, Winfield
1-800-991-3233 or (250) 766-4086

Wildways Adventures Sports Tours

1925 Highway #3, Christina Lake
1-800-663-6561 or ph/fax (250) 447-6561

Landowners

Penticton Indian Band Administration

Westhill Dr., Penticton, B.C.
(250) 493-0048

Coldwater Indian Band

2249 Quilchena, Merritt, B.C.
(250) 378-6174
Fax (250) 378-5351

Lower Nicola Band Administration Office

#73 Shulus, Highway #8, Lower Nicola, B.C.
(250) 378-5157

Nooaitch Band Administration

(250) 378-6141

Shakan Band Administration

2090 Coutlee, Merritt, B.C.
(250) 378-5410

Topographical Maps

Map Suppliers
Nanaimo Maps & Charts
8 Church Street
Nanaimo, BC V9R 5H4
1-800-665-2513
Tel (604)754-2513 Fax 754-2313
1:50,000

Map Town
640 - 6 Ave SW
Calgary, AB T2P 0S4
Tel (403) 266-2241
Fax (403) 266-2356

1:250,000
Kettle Valley Railway
92 H Hope
82 E Penticton

C&W Railway
82 E Penticton
82 F Nelson

NK&S Railway
92 H Hope
92 I Ashcroft

VV&E Railway
92 H Hope
82 E Penticton
NM 11-10 Okanagan

Midway to Penticton
82 E/2 Greenwood
82 E/3 Osoyoos
82 E/6 Beaverdell
82 E/11 Wilkinson Creek
82 E/14 Kelowna
82 E/12 Summerland
82 E/5 Penticton
82 E/4 Keremeos

Penticton to Princeton
82 E/12 Summerland
92 H/9 Bandeir
92 H/8 Hedley
92 H/7 Princeton

Princeton to Brookmere
92 H/7 Princeton
92 H/10 Tulameen
92 H/15 Aspen Grove

Brookmere to Merritt
92 H/15 Aspen Grove
92 I/2 Merritt

Brookmere to Hope
92 H/15 Aspen Grove
92 H/14 Boston Bar
92 H/11 Spuzzum
92 H/6 Hope

C&W Railway
82 F/5 Castlegar
82 E/8 Deer Park
82 E/1 Grand Forks
82E/2 Greenwood

NK&S Railway
92 I/2 Merritt
92 I/3 Prospect Creek
92 I/6 Spences Bridge

VV&E Railway
92 H/7 Princeton
92 H/8 Hedley
92 H/1 Ashnola River
92 E/4 Keremeos
82 E/3 Osoyoos
82 E/2 Greenwood

USA Maps (VV&E Railway)
1:25,000   7 x 15' Series
48119 - H1-T   M-025
48119 - H3-T   M-025
48119 - H5-T   M-025

Services

Following is a list of some services you may find useful when cycling or planning your trip. This is not a comprehensive list or a recommendation of any particular facility.

Bicycle Services

Sun Country Cycle (250) 493-0686
533 Main Street, Penticton

The Bike Barn   (250) 492-4140
300 Westminster Avenue, Penticton

High Country Sports   (250) 494-5050
10120 Main, Summerland

Kelowna Cycle   (250) 762-0660
2949 Pandosy, Kelowna

Ry-Dan Sports (250) 378-3939
2049 Quilchena Ave., Merritt

Backroad Bike Shop (250) 295-3735
Nicola Ave. & 5th Street, Tulameen

Silver Barn Bike & Board 1-800-667-1196 or (250) 442-8006
Highway #3 West, Grand Forks

Wildways Adventure Sports & Tours 1-800-663-6561 or (250) 447-6561
Johnson Road & Highway #3, Christina Lake

Airlines

Canadian Airlines (Penticton)   (250) 492-0614
Air Canada/Air BC (Penticton)   (250) 492-2165
Air Canada/Air BC (within B.C.) 1-800-663-3721
Air Canada/Air BC (from USA)   1-800-663-8868
Westjet Airlines 1-800-538-5696
Greyhound Airlines 1-800-661-8747
Both airlines provide daily service to Castlegar, Penticton and Kelowna.

Greyhound Bus Lines 1-800-663-8868

Penticton   (250) 492-2606
Provides bus service to most towns en route.

Via Rail

From Canada 1-800-561-8630
From USA   1-800-561-3949
Provides rail service to Edmonton, Jasper, Kamloops, Boston Bar,
Ashcroft, Hope and Vancouver.

Car Rentals

Avis Rent-A-Car   (250) 493-8133
Budget Rent-A-Car   (250) 493-0212
Tilden Rent-A-Car   (250) 493-7288

Travel Infocentres

Midway	449-2614	
Rock Creek	446-2455	
Penticton	493-4055	fax 492-6119
Oliver	498-6321	fax 498-3156
Osoyoos	495-7142	fax 495-6161
Summerland	494-2686	fax 494-4039
Princeton	295-3103	fax 295-3255
Merritt	378-2281	fax 378-6485
Hope (604)	869-2021	fax 869-2160
Castlegar	365-6313	fax 365-5778
Christina Lake	447-6161	
Grand Forks	442-2833	
Greenwood	445-6777	

B.C. Wine Institute (Kelowna)   1-800-661-2294 / (250) 762-4887

Okanagan Wine Tours   (250) 490-9898

Weather Forecasts (Penticton)   (250) 492–6991

Grocery Stores:

Castlegar, Christina Lake, Grand Forks, Greenwood, Midway, Rock Creek, Westbridge, Beaverdell, Penticton, Kaleden, Okanagan Falls, Oliver, Osoyoos, Summerland, Osprey Lake (3 Lakes General Store), Princeton, Tulameen, Hope, Nicola, Merritt, Lower Nicola, Spences Bridge.

Laundromats:

Castlegar: Bel-Air Laundry, 632-18th Street, 365-5145
Christina Lake: Christina Lake Laundry, 19 West Lake, 447-6422
Grand Forks: Sunshine Valley Laundromat, 7344-3rd Street, 442-2315
Greenwood: Motherload Laundry, corner of Gold St.(Highway #3) and Washington St., 445-6763
Chute Lake: coin laundry at Chute Lake Resort
Penticton: The Laundry Basket, 976 W. Eckhardt Ave., 493-7899
Osoyoos: Lakeview Plaza Laundry, 8401-93 St., 495-7577
Pete's Laundry, 7301-62 Ave., 495-3295
Princeton: 148 Bridge St. & Halliford Ave., 295-7542
Tulameen: corner of 2nd Street & Otter Road
Merritt: laundry/showers, across from Coldwater Hotel on Quilchena Ave.
Clean Gene's coin laundry, 2749 - Nicola Ave. (east end of avenue)
Hope: coin laundry located in Midtown Mall

Emergency Medical Services: 1-800-461-9911

In case of any emergency, dial this phone number and a dispatcher will best assist you in obtaining the emergency service you require.

Hospitals are located at Castlegar, Grand Forks, Penticton, Oliver, Summerland, Princeton, Merritt and Hope.

Suggested References

Barlee, N. L., *Gold Creeks and Ghost Towns.* Canada West Magazine, Box 995, Summerland, Western Heritage Supply, Box 208, Burnaby 1, Nov. 1980

Basque, Garnet, *Ghost Towns & Mining Camps of the Boundary Country,* Sunfire Publications Ltd., Langley 1992

Blake, Don, *Blakeburn, From Dust to Dust*

Boundary Historical Society
4th Report 1964, 5th Report 1967, 9th Report 1983, 10th Report 1985, 12th Report 1992

McCulloch, Andrew, *A History of the Kettle Valley Railway*

Okanagan Historical Society, 13th Report 1950, 25th Report

Sanford, Barrie, *McCulloch's Wonder*, Whitecap Books, Vancouver 1989

Sanford, Barrie, *Steel Rails and Iron Men*, Whitecap Books, Vancouver 1990

Shewchuck, Murphy, *Backroads Explorer Vol. 2: Similkameen and South Okanagan*, Hancock House, Surrey, 1988

Shewchuck, Murphy, *Coquihalla Country*, Sonotek Publishing, Merritt, 1990

Turnbull, Elise G., *Ghost Towns and Drowned Towns of the West Kootenay,* Heritage House Publishing Company Ltd., Surrey 1988

Turner, Robert D., *Steam on the Kettle Valley,* Sono Nis Press, Victoria 1995

White, John, *Driving the Kettle Valley Railway, Field Maps and Notes,* John White 1996, 344 Oxford Drive, Port Moody, BC V3H 1T2, (604) 936-2367 email jwhite@planeteer.com

Wisnicki, Mike, *Over the Hill, A Guide to Mountain Bike Rides in the Grand Forks Area*, Ground Forks Publications, Grand Forks 1994

Vander Plas, Rob, *Mountain Bike Maintenance,* Bicycle Books, 1989

Web Sites

Check out the **author's** web site for updates and changes.
www.planet.eon.net/~dan/

Check out **Rocky Mountain Books'** site for more outdoor recreation guides.
www.rmbooks.com